Herbs

for cooking

By

ROGER PHILLIPS
& MARTYN RIX

Research by Alison Rix
Design Jill Bryan & Debby Curry

Acknowledgements

We would like to thank the following gardens and
herb suppliers for allowing us to visit them and
photograph their plants:
The Royal Horticultural Society's Garden, Wisley,
Surrey; Cambridge University Botanic Garden;
Gravetye Manor; Arley Hall: Ventnor Botanic
Garden, Isle of Wight; Portmeirion Gardens, North
Wales; Barnsley House Garden; The Ballymaloe
Cookery School Garden; Eden Croft Herb Garden;
Hollington's Herb Garden; Eccleston Square
Gardens; Villandry

Among others who have helped in one way or another
we would like to thank: Rosemary Verey,
Joy Larkcom, Marilyn Inglis, Anne & Tom Thatcher,
Darina Allen, Jan & Derick Curry and Roger Poulett.

First published 1998 by Pan
an imprint of Macmillan Publishers Limited
25 Eccleston Place, London SW1W 9NF
and Basingstoke
Associated companies throughout the world
ISBN 0-330-35546-5
Copyright in the text and illustrations
© Roger Phillips and Martyn Rix
The right of the authors to be identified as the
authors
of this work has been asserted by them in
accordance with the Copyright, Designs and
Patents Act 1988.

Colour Reproduction by Aylesbury Studios Ltd.
Printed by Butler and Tanner Ltd. Frome, Somerset

Contents

A group of herbs showing contrasting colour and foliage

Introduction

Herbs – defined as plants whose leaves, flowers, stems, seeds and roots are used for culinary or medicinal purposes – have been used by man to enhance his food from the very earliest times. There are many historical records of the gathering and cultivation of herbs for these purposes, and the culinary uses and cultivation of herbs continue to be of interest to those who enjoy gardening and good food. The old Herbals contain much of interest too, and some of them have been reprinted in facsimile, making them available to the general reader. In this book we focus on the herbs useful for cooking, their characteristics, growing requirements and their uses.

There are an enormous number of culinary herbs, and it is impossible to illustrate every one in a small book, so we have selected those that are easy to grow, and of real use in the kitchen; not only edible, but truly palatable. In one or two cases we have included herbs that do not strictly fulfil these criteria, but which are so well known that their absence would seem odd; the exception to this is Rue, which we have omitted as it can actually cause harm to some people.

Choosing Herbs

We have attempted to give a wide selection of good plants, so that the reader can make an informed choice based on preference and the requirements of the plant. To achieve success, you should accept that you are unlikely to be able to grow every type of herb; some prefer poor, rocky soil, while others need good deep, moist earth to flourish and not all gardeners can provide both types of habitat. If your life is busy and time at a premium, avoid those plants that need constant watering, pinching out and staking. Climate is also important (*see opposite*), and lack of a long warm summer, for example, will sometimes affect a plant's ability to produce seed, which might stop you from trying some of the spices described at the end of the book. The ability to provide greenhouse or other protection in the winter

Golden
Marjoram

Herb garden on the Isle of Mull

can make a difference too. Even if you have no garden, you will still be able to grow many herbs in pots on a balcony or windowsill, and we have recommended some that do well in containers.

Gardening should be fun and a herb garden can be very attractive when a variety of plants is grown. We have therefore included not only the indispensable herbs such as mint and parsley, but also a few of the more unusual varieties, such as Basil 'Purple Ruffles', to provide a challenge. A decorative variety – for example, 'Icterina', which is a variegated sage – can often be as useful as the better known type and prettier to look at.

States in mind. However, differences in climate will mean that there will be slightly different requirements with regard to protection from extremes of temperature, time of sowing, harvesting and so on. Where applicable, the natural habitat of the species has been given in the belief that this will help the gardener to provide suitable growing conditions. The idea is simple; if the plant is native to a hot, rocky hillside in Turkey it will need a well-drained, sunny site in the garden. Conversely, a herb that prefers boggy patches of shady woodland is unlikely to thrive in the scorching heat of an open border. Once this simple principle is grasped you should have no trouble!

Growing Herbs

Horticulture is an inexact science, and there are no general rules for growing herbs; planting details will be found under individual entries in the following pages. The plants have been chosen with gardeners throughout northern Europe and the United

Herb Gardens

Much has already been written on the subject of herb gardens, their design and planting. The best way to get ideas is to look at as many gardens as you can (*see page 93*), and decide which elements please your eye and suit your plot and pocket. There are no hard and fast rules, unless you wish to reconstruct an historically accurate design, but there are a few commonsense points to be made. The first is that herbs can be grown in any part of the garden and do not have to be corralled in the herb or kitchen garden; some striking plants, such as bronze fennel, look wonderful in herbaceous borders. Secondly, a herb garden tends to be most useful sited close to the house. Thirdly, bear in mind the logistics of harvesting herbs – narrow borders often make this easier. A final point to remember is that some herbs are very invasive and when planning your garden, you should try to devise a way of containing such plants; a common solution is to divide a bed into sections using stones, bricks or boards.

Using Herbs in the Kitchen

Although the way you use herbs in cooking is mainly a matter of personal preference, certain herbs have become associated over the years with particular foods. Horseradish, for example, is often used in a piquant sauce for beef or for oily smoked fish such as mackerel, while sage and thyme constitute the traditional flavouring of stuffing for poultry, and fennel and dill enhance the flavour of fish such as salmon. The leaves of many herbs, such as coriander and parsley, are best used fresh, while others, such as Bay *Laurus nobilis*, develop a better flavour after drying. Unless otherwise stated, leaves may

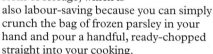

Variegated sage

be dried on newspaper (in the sun, preferably) and stored (on the stalk if possible) in tall glass jars in a darkish place.

Another method of keeping herbs is to freeze them, which is sometimes preferable to drying as the leaves retain more of their colour and flavour. Herbs such as parsley benefit from this form of storage, which is also labour-saving because you can simply crunch the bag of frozen parsley in your hand and pour a handful, ready-chopped straight into your cooking.

Herbs in History

Although we use culinary herbs nowadays simply because we like the various flavours, it is worth remembering that in the past they were often used to disguise the unpleasant taste of preserved or slightly spoiled meat and fish; this explains why some strongly flavoured herbs gained a popularity that seems inexplicable to us. The earliest-known cookery book, written by the Roman Apicius, has been translated from Latin and republished and called the *Roman Cookery Book* (Harrap, 1958). From it we learn how much the Romans relied on herbs and spices to flavour their complicated recipes; a sauce for oysters and shellfish, for example, calls for lovage, parsley, dry mint, bay leaf and cumin. This heavy reliance on herbs and spices continued throughout the succeeding centuries, and there are numerous references to their use and cultivation.

A Treatise on the Noble Art and Mystery of Cookery by Charles Carter, *c.* 1740, indicates how important herbs were in the 18th-century English kitchen. During this period it was common for people to grow their own herbs, and this continued to be the case until the early 20th century when people increasingly found it easier to buy food rather than grow it themselves.

Herbs associate well with many other plants

Many gardeners plant herbs to attract bees

Herbs merit little attention in many cook books published during the war years, with little reference to any but the most common herbs, such as parsley, sage and thyme, but interest in a wider range of herbs was again aroused during the late 1950s and 1960s by writers such as Elizabeth David who had lived and worked in Europe, where the use of herbs was still prevalent. On the other side of the Atlantic, the American triumvirate of Child, Bertholle and Beck who wrote *Mastering the Art of French Cooking* (Knopf, 1970) inspired a similar revival. Jane Grigson also did much to encourage cooks to use fresh produce; her books on fruit and vegetables (*see page 93*) are classics.

There are now many specialist suppliers and growers of herbs from whom plants can be bought for growing at home. These days fresh-cut herbs and herbs in pots can be purchased with ease in many stores and supermarkets.

Using this Book

This volume is written for amateur gardeners, not botanists, so the use of technical terms has been kept to a minimum. There is a glossary (*see page 92*) which explains the few words in the text that may require clarification. The herbs are grouped together according to type, so that, for example, seed-bearing plants are found next to each other, and those which look similar can be compared. Both common and Latin names of plants are given in the text and in the index so that ordering plants from catalogues is as simple as possible.

White sage is attractive as well as useful

Caraway Thyme *Thymus herba-barona*

Thymus doerfleri 'Bressingham Pink'

Thymus 'Doone Valley'

Thyme

Thymes are small shrubby perennial plants native to Europe and the Mediterranean region, growing in dry stony soil on heath and downlands, and grassy upland places. Most thymes are small creeping plants with mats of woody stems clothed in numerous small, aromatic leaves. It is these leaves, picked fresh or dried and kept in airtight jars, which are used in cooking. The small flowers are very attractive, and thymes are frequently grown for their ornamental attributes.

Thymus doerfleri

Thyme is an essential ingredient of *bouquet garni* and is also used in soups, stews, stuffings and marinades. Turkish cooking uses it as an accompaniment to grilled lamb, or, more exotically, in *Borek* (a puff pastry envelope) filled with meat. *The Greens Cook Book* has an excellent recipe for butter-fried onions with vinegar and thyme which calls for several branches of thyme.

There are about 60 European species, and not surprisingly, a certain amount of confusion over some of the names. Those found wild in Britain include *Thymus polytrichus* subsp. *britannicus*, *Thymus serpyllum* and *Thymus pulegioides*. Large numbers of cultivars have been raised from the various species and these are more commonly grown in herb gardens than their wild relatives, chiefly because their flavour tends to be more pronounced. The species and cultivars listed here are available from nurseries and garden centres, and, where applicable, are listed under their common names.

PLANTING HELP Thymes can be grown in the garden, in containers outdoors and inside on a sunny windowsill. They are sometimes planted as a seat, as the crushed leaves give off a wonderful scent. Most of the mat-forming varieties (such as Caraway Thyme or 'September') will also do well when planted in cracks in paving or in gravel paths where they do not mind being trodden on. Thymes generally prefer light slightly sandy, well-drained soil in a sunny position. Do not overwater, particularly in winter. They are usually very low-growing and extremely hardy. Most thymes are easily propagated from softwood cuttings taken in the spring, or in the case of a few varieties, from minute seeds. To take cuttings, snip shoots to about 2½–2¾in (6–7cm) and grow on in compost

THYME

The thyme garden at Hollington Nurseries

made up of more or less equal parts of peat, sand, bark and grit. All thymes will benefit from an annual trim after flowering to prevent legginess.

Thymus doerfleri A low-growing, mat-forming shrub native to Albania, with unusual thin grey woolly leaves and soft pink or purple flowers borne on stems up to 3in (8cm) tall. It dislikes excessive moisture and will not tolerate waterlogging, especially in winter.
'Bressingham Pink' Mat-forming and grows to about the same size as *Thymus doefleri*, but unlike its parent, it has green leaves. The flowers are pale mauvy pink and appear in summer. It needs well-drained conditions to survive winter. Hardy to 10°F (−12°C), US zones 8–10.

Caraway Thyme *Thymus herba-barona* A mat-forming plant that grows to only about ¾in (2cm) tall and 8in (20cm) wide, it puts out arching shoots that root on contact with the soil (these can be detached to form new plants). Native to Corsica and Sardinia where it is known as *herba-barona*. The dark green leaves are extremely small and the rose pink or mauve flowers appear in midsummer. The scent is a curious mixture of caraway and thyme, which combines well with game or other red meats, such as venison. Hardy to 20°F (−6°C), US zones 9–10.

***Thymus* 'Doone Valley'** Possibly a form of Lemon Thyme *T.* × *citriodorus*, this attractive creeping variety grows up to 3in (8cm) tall and 8in (20cm) wide. It has round, lemon-scented, dark green leaves splashed with gold. Its flowers are purple and appear in summer. Not the first choice for cooking but quite useful and very pretty in the garden. Hardy to 20°F (−6°C), US zones 9–10.

Thymus comosus Native to Greece and Turkey, this species has a low bushy habit of growth. The rose pink or purplish flowers appear in midsummer and are borne on stems about 5in (12cm) tall. Hardy to 20°F (−6°C), US zones 9–10.

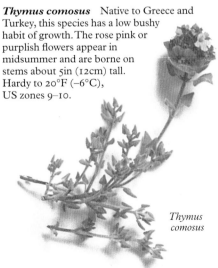

Thymus comosus

9

THYME

Thymus vulgaris 'Silver Posie'

Garden or Common Thyme *Thymus vulgaris*

Wild Thyme *Thymus polytrichus* subsp. *britannicus*

Garden or **Common Thyme** *Thymus vulgaris*
As its name implies, this is the most well-known thyme. A low-growing evergreen shrub native to the W Mediterranean region where it grows on dry gravelly soil; it is also commonly cultivated throughout Europe. It grows to about 10in (25cm) tall and nearly as wide, producing spikes of numerous small pale mauve flowers during the summer. Snip off the dead flowers to encourage new growth, or grow as an annual from seed. The addition of a little chalk or limestone to the soil will help it thrive. If really happy, the plant will sometimes reward you with self-sown seedlings which can be transplanted; or it can be increased by cuttings or by division. One of the more strongly flavoured thymes, it is most commonly used for *bouquet garni* and for stuffing meat.

There are several varieties of Common Thyme, and one of the prettiest is **'Silver Posie'** with silver variegated leaves and pale mauve flowers. It grows up to about 12in (30cm) tall and 8in (20cm) wide. The leaves have a good taste and smell. In our experience it does well in indifferent soils and is reliably hardy to 0°F (−18°C), US zones 7–10.

Wild Thyme *Thymus polytrichus* subsp. *britannicus*
Grows wild in Britain and N Europe and has been subject to many name changes (previously called *Thymus drucei* and *T. praecox* subsp. *arcticus*), causing confusion. The small dark green leaves are mildly scented and the pinkish mauve flowers are carried in a dense spike, from late spring on. It is a creeping plant, growing on dry stony ground. Hardy to 10°F (−12°C), US zones 8–10.

Lemon Thyme *Thymus × citriodorus*

Lemon Thyme *Thymus × citriodorus*   A loose bush that grows up to 12in (30cm) tall and 8in (20cm) wide and has broad lemon-scented leaves. Deep pink flowers appear a little later than some of the other thymes, and if picked when in flower it dries well, retaining its flavour for many months. Lemon Thyme prefers a richer soil than most of the other varieties shown here, but care must still be taken to protect it from excessive wet and cold. Like Common Thyme (*see page 10*) it is increased by cuttings or division. The leaves have a slightly milder flavour than other thymes and it is used to flavour baked custard. Deborah Madison uses Lemon Thyme in a potato gratin with olives. Hardy to 20°F (−6°C), US zones 9–10.

A selection of the numerous varieties of Lemon Thyme (which are normally as hardy as the species) is listed below:

'Bertram Anderson' ('Anderson's Gold', 'E. B. Anderson')   A small mounded bush that grows to about 4in (10cm) tall and twice as wide, and has golden green leaves. The pinkish mauve flowers make an attractive feature in the herb garden, and its mild flavour is useful in salads.

Thymus × citriodorus 'Bertram Anderson'

'Silver Queen' Grows up to about 12in (30cm) tall and about 8in (20cm) wide. It has creamy silver variegations on the rather grey leaves, which have a pronounced lemon scent. Very good with light fish or poultry dishes. Hardy to 20°F (−6°C), US zones 9–10.

Many herbs grow well in containers; seen here is *Thymus × citriodorus* 'Silver Queen'

Thymus hyemalis

Woolly Thyme *Thymus pseudolanuginosus*

Thymus pulegioides

Thymus hyemalis   Native to Spain, this species is similar to Common Thyme, but the leaves are greyer. Hardy to 0°F (–18°C), US zones 7–10.

Thymus pulegioides   This species grows up to 4in (10cm) tall and twice as wide and is native to Europe, including the southeast of England where it grows in calcareous areas. It will be happiest if you add a little chalk to the soil. The broad dark green leaves are very aromatic and the flowers are bright pinkish purple. It is both attractive and useful in the kitchen. Hardy to 0°F (–18°C), US zones 7–10.

Thymus quinquecostatus   Our rarity in the thyme section, this creeper from the deserts of Mongolia and from Japan will be a focus of attention in your herb garden. The decorative rose pink flowers are borne in clusters on stems about 4in (10cm) tall. Not easy to obtain in Britain at the moment but well known in the USA. Hardy to 0°F (–18°C), US zones 7–10.

Thymus serpyllum   Like *Thymus polytrichus* subsp. *britannicus*, this species is also known as Wild Thyme in Britain because it grows here, but it is a confusing epithet as all species grow wild somewhere in the world. This very aromatic creeping shrub is found throughout N Europe on dry stony ground. Hardy to 0°F (–18°C), US zones 7–10. It has a woody root and long creeping stems, and from these arise flowering stems to about 4in (10cm) tall with dense clusters of tiny

Thymus quinquecostatus at the RHS Garden, Wisley

THYME

Thymus serpyllum is native of much of Northern Europe, and has given rise to many cultivars

pinkish mauve flowers. It has long been valued for its culinary use, as an aid to digesting fatty foods and for its antiseptic properties.

Thymus serpyllum has given rise to over 40 cultivars, of which a small selection is illustrated here. Many of these varieties are very similar to one another and there is a certain amount of confusion over the names, which is frustrating if you are trying to obtain a particular variety.

'Lemon Curd' This has lemon-scented grey green leaves and pale mauve flowers and is a creeping variety like its parent. The small leaves are bright green and smell slightly of lemon.

'September' As its name suggests, this late-flowering form produces tiny purple flowers from August to October. It forms a low-growing mat which spreads up to 2ft (60cm) in favourable conditions. Good for gravel or for growing in gaps in paving.

Woolly Thyme *Thymus pseudolanuginosus*
A mat-forming species of unknown origin, this plant likes dry conditions and needs very little soil. The pale pink flowers are produced throughout the summer, but its main feature is its woolly grey leaves. Hardy to 0°F (−18°C), US zones 7–10.

Thymus serpyllum 'September'

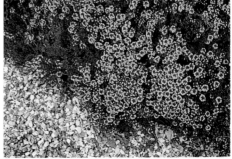

Thymus serpyllum 'Lemon Curd'

Basil

Common Basil

From a cook's point of view, basil must be rated among the top ten herbs. It has a very distinctive aromatic taste and smell, and is widely used in Italian cooking. It can be turned into pesto sauce or preserved in oil, and recipes for these methods of using it are given by Elizabeth David in her excellent book *Italian Food*. There are numerous good recipes using basil; Deborah Madison has a delicious one for filo pastry filled with grated zucchini and basil, and another for summer potato soup with tomatoes and basil, while Elizabeth David suggests trying it with duck.

Many people find that the flavour of basil complements that of tomatoes perfectly, which is handy as both are at their peak around the same time. In fact, my most successful attempts at growing this sometimes tricky herb have always been when growing it with, or next to, tomato plants. It also makes an attractive plant for the windowsill (in colder climes) or outside if you are lucky enough to live somewhere warm.

The exact origins of basil are unknown, although it is thought to come from SE Asia and possibly India. It is known that basil has been cultivated in Europe for a very long time; there are early references to it in ancient Greek and Roman literature. At the Roman palace of Fishbourne, West Sussex, England, there is a re-creation of a Roman garden and basil can be seen there.

There are many varieties of basil available and the choice seems to increase all the time. The US lists contain large numbers of different named types, but not all of these are available in Britain. For culinary purposes the Common or Sweet Basil is the most useful, while Bush Basil is probably the best for growing in pots. For subtly different flavours you could try Cinnamon, Lemon or Liquorice basils.

PLANTING HELP   Although basil can be grown as a perennial plant in warm countries, in cooler climates it is treated as an annual. Seed of several varieties is now available. When grown as

Common or Sweet Basil *Ocimum basilicum* is one of the best of all culinary herbs

BASIL

Basil 'Cinnamon'

Lettuce-leaved Basil

an annual from seed, it makes a small bush 12in (30cm) tall, whereas outside in favourable conditions it can grow to about 2ft (60cm). The seeds are best sown during the late winter or early spring in good seed compost and kept at a temperature above 68°F (20°C). After germinating (which takes 2–3 weeks) they can be grown on until large enough to handle. All basils are prone to damping off; avoid this problem by sowing seeds very thinly and water only during dry weather in the morning. Carefully transplant the seedlings into small pots and gradually harden off; do not be tempted to plant them outside until all risk of frost has passed. Plant them in good (but not manured), well-drained soil and give them a really warm, sunny, sheltered spot in the garden. If you plan to grow basil plants on your windowsill, pot them on (preferably in well-drained soil with some sand or grit) and water carefully. By picking off the young tips for culinary use you will help retain its bushy habit, but you should also remove any flowering shoots to ensure a continuous supply of fresh young leaves. We have found the purple and more tropical basils much trickier to grow and even more liable to damping off than the common green variety. Careful watering is important if they are to make good-sized plants.

Common, Genovese or **Sweet Basil** *Ocimum basilicum* Depending on climate, this species can be either an annual bushy plant that grows to about 12in (30cm), or a perennial that eventually reaches to about 3½ft (1m) high. The strongly scented leaves are a glossy light green; the flowers are white, sometimes tinged with pale purple. This is the most popular and easily obtainable of the basils and the best variety for making pesto. It is often sold as a pot plant in the salad section of supermarkets or delicatessens, in nurseries and

garden centres. You can also grow it yourself from seed. Snip off the leaf tips for cooking and cut off any shoots that are about to flower as this will keep the plant producing healthy leaves for longer. Prefers a warm place. Hardy to 32°F (0°C), US zone 10.

'Cinnamon' A pink-flowered variety of Common Basil, this has greenish bronze leaves tinged with purple, which actually smell of cinnamon when crushed. Like most basils, it can be used to add piquancy to green salads or dressings, and also associates well with curry. Hardy to 32°F (0°C), US zone 10.

Basil 'Cinnamon'

Lettuce-leaved Basil *Ocimum basilicum* 'Neapolitanum' This variety grows to about 18in (45cm) and is similar to the common Sweet Basil, but has much larger leaves and a slightly stronger flavour. It requires ample sun and warmth.

Holy or Sacred Basil *Ocimum tenuiflorum*

Bush or **Greek Basil** *Ocimum basilicum* var. *minimum* This is now thought to be a small-leaved form of Common Basil. It makes a compact bush up to about 12in (30cm) tall and is particularly useful for growing in a pot. The ovate leaves are very small, less than ⅓in (1cm) long; the small white flowers should be snipped off if you want to continue to use the leaves in cooking. If growing this on your kitchen windowsill, you will also reap the benefit of its properties as a fly repellent. Hardy to 32°F (0°C), US zone 10.

Holy or **Sacred Basil** *Ocimum tenuiflorum* (syn. *O. sanctum)* Native to India and Malaysia where it is considered a sacred herb by the Hindus. In the wild it can grow up to 3½ft (1m) tall, but in cultivation it normally makes a compact bush of about 12in (30cm). The green leaves have serrated edges and are sometimes tinged with purple; both

stems and leaves are covered with short hairs. The pinkish mauve flowers are carrried in whorls on the flowering stems and the whole plant is strongly aromatic. Hardy to 32°F (0°C), US zone 10.

'Liquorice Basil' This variety has purple stems and glossy mid- to darkish green leaves, making a fine plant. It smells strongly of liquorice, and in small quantities combines well with fish. Hardy to 32°F (0°C), US zone 10.

'Purple Basil' *Ocimum basilicum* var. *purpureum* The purple-leaved variety of Common Basil is known and sold under this name; another form, distributed under the name 'Dark Opal' seems to be identical. Its scent is similar to ordinary basil, but with an undertone of cloves. Very pretty little flowers of pale mauvy pink and the dark purple leaves provide an interesting contrast of colour in

Bush or Greek Basil

'Purple Basil'

'Red Basil'

'Thai Basil'

Lemon Basil *Ocimum basilicum* var. *citriodorum*

'Liquorice Basil'

green salads; it also enhances egg and pasta dishes. Hardy to 32°F (0°C), US zone 10.

'Purple Ruffles'
Similar to 'Purple Basil', but the leaves are larger and have ruffled edges when mature and the flavour is milder. This basil is not easy to keep and is only really worth growing if you are an avid collector of different varieties, although the leaves do look very pretty in green salads. Hardy to 32°F (0°C), US zone 10.

'Purple Ruffles'

'Red Basil' A purple-leaved variety which seems more or less identical to 'Purple Basil', although the flowers are a brighter pink. Hardy to 32°F (0°C), US zone 10.

'Thai Basil' or **'Horapha'** Has a strong aniseed scent and can be used to flavour curries and other Thai dishes; it is also good with pork. It grows to

about 16in (40cm) tall and has greenish-brown leaves and pink flowers with purplish bracts. It seems to tolerate very hot dry conditions. Hardy to 32°F (0°C), US zone 10.

Lemon Basil *Ocimum basilicum* var. *citriodorum*
As its name suggests, this basil has bright green lemon-scented leaves and white lemon-scented flowers; it goes well with chicken and fish. Paul Bertolli in his *Chez Panisse Cooking*, suggests adding it to lobster salad or fish and shellfish soup. Hardy to 32°F (0°C), US zone 10.

Mint

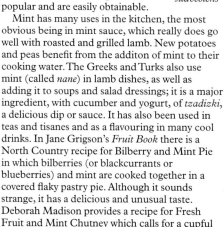

There are about 25 species and numerous varieties of mint and the names are hopelessly muddled. However, this is not a worry from the cook's point of view, as there are a number of varieties which have long been popular and are easily obtainable.

Bowles Mint
Mentha suaveolens

Mint has many uses in the kitchen, the most obvious being in mint sauce, which really does go well with roasted and grilled lamb. New potatoes and peas benefit from the additon of mint to their cooking water. The Greeks and Turks also use mint (called *nane*) in lamb dishes, as well as adding it to soups and salad dressings; it is a major ingredient, with cucumber and yogurt, of *tzadizki*, a delicious dip or sauce. It has also been used in teas and tisanes and as a flavouring in many cool drinks. In Jane Grigson's *Fruit Book* there is a North Country recipe for Bilberry and Mint Pie in which bilberries (or blackcurrants or blueberries) and mint are cooked together in a covered flaky pastry pie. Although it sounds strange, it has a delicious and unusual taste. Deborah Madison provides a recipe for Fresh Fruit and Mint Chutney which calls for a cupful of mint leaves; this chutney is an ideal accompaniment to curry.

Most species of mint originate from Asia and southern Europe where there is a long history of their use in the kitchen. The Greeks and Romans were partial to the taste; it is thought that the mint used by the Romans was probably Water Mint (*Mentha aquatica*) which grows wild near streams and ponds (*see page 21*).

PLANTING HELP Most mints are creeping plants which spread freely if given the chance; it is usually wise to restrain mint by planting next to a wall or path so it cannot rampage through the bed! Some people go so far as to plant it in a bottomless container, such as an old bucket or box, to try to keep it under control. Mint grows in warm well-drained soils, but needs plenty of moisture so is best given a spot in rich soil in partial shade where the soil will not dry out quickly. Mints are freely available from nurseries and garden centres and are also easy to propagate by pulling off rooted runners and replanting where required. After a few years, you will find that the plants are failing to thrive; at this point, prepare a new area for replacement plants, digging in plenty of manure. Some mints suffer from mildew and rust, but it is unwise to spray culinary plants. In any case these afflictions are not fatal to the plant, so just cut off the affected shoots and burn them; in my experience these diseases will disappear by the

Mint is very invasive, and is often grown in containers to restrain it. Seen here in Mexico

Apple Mint *Mentha suaveolens* in the background

next spring. Most mints are very hardy (*see individual entries*), and while they die down in the coldest part of the winter, they do not disappear for long. As we write (early February) young shoots of Apple Mint are appearing in our garden.

Apple Mint or **Round-leaved Mint** *Mentha suaveolens*   A round-leaved form that grows to about 2½ft (75cm) tall and has a stout, furry stem that smells of apples and mint. The slightly furry, wrinkled rounded leaves are directly attached to the main stem, and the lilac flowers are borne in dense spikes at the top of the stems. For a good moist soil in sun or shade, but beware, as it is very invasive. Hardy to 0°F (−18°C), US zones 7–10.

Bowles Mint *Mentha suaveolens*   This form is derived from Apple Mint and was named after the great gardener Edward Augustus Bowles (1865–1954) who considered this the best form for making mint sauce. It is a vigorous variety, eventually growing to 3½ft (1m) tall and has large, furry, stalkless leaves with serrated edges, and

large spikes of lilac flowers. This plant wilts very quickly once picked – after only 15 minutes it curls up sadly, so you will not find it in your local supermarket. Plant in good moist soil, in sun or shade. Hardy to 0°F (−18°C), US zones 7–10.

Apple Mint

Corn Mint *Mentha arvensis*

Pineapple Mint *Mentha suaveolens* 'Variegata'
This variety of Apple Mint has cream and green
variegated leaves and a very slight scent of
pineapple. It grows to 2ft (60cm) tall and prefers a
rich moist soil in partial shade. The leaves are
good chopped and added to salads and fruit
salads; it is attractive when added to cool summer
drinks. Frequent picking of the young stems will
promote fresh growth. Hardy to 0°F (−18°C), US
zones 7–10.

Corn Mint *Mentha arvensis*   A variable plant that
grows up to 2ft (60cm) tall, it is widely distributed
through Britain, Europe and parts of N Asia and
Japan, where it grows in arable fields and
seasonally damp places. The oval-shaped leaves
are hairy on both sides, and the lilac or pink (and
occasionally white) flowers are borne in whorls up
the stem. Hardy to 0°F (−18°C), US zones 7–10.

Pennyroyal or **Pudding Grass** *Mentha pulegium*
Native to much of Europe, this is one of the
smallest mints; a low-growing creeping plant that
seldom reaches more than 6in (15cm). It has tiny
bright green peppermint-scented leaves, and lilac

Pineapple Mint *Mentha suaveolens* 'Variegata'

Pennyroyal *Mentha pulegium*

Water Mint in flower

flowers appearing in late spring. It is included here mainly as a curiosity, as Pennyroyal is seldom used in the kitchen these days due to its strong, bitter taste, but it was much used in the past as an ingredient in otherwise bland puddings and as a tea. Pennyroyal creeps along the surface of the soil and roots easily at points where it is in direct contact with the earth, so it is extremely easy to propagate. Simply dig up small clumps in spring and replant where required, or put into pots (it is quite invasive). If possible, mix a little sand into the compost when you pot it up. Hardy to 0°F (−18°C), US zones 7–10.

Water Mint *Mentha aquatica*

Pineapple Mint

Water Mint *Mentha aquatica*   This attractive mint grows up to about 2ft (60cm) tall and is found growing wild in Britain and Europe on the margins of streams and ponds, therefore it must be given a very wet place in the garden. It gives off a lovely, sweet, peppermint scent when crushed. The perfect use for this plant is in the cooking water of new potatoes. The softly hairy leaves have slightly serrated edges and the stems are often reddish purple; lilac flowers are produced throughout the summer. Hardy to 0°F (−18°C), US zones 7–10.

Mentha × verticillata This hybrid between Corn Mint and Water Mint is very variable, although it is usually more robust than Corn Mint. It grows up to about 3ft (90cm) tall and bears whorls of lilac flowers. It is quite commonly found growing wild throughout Britain and Europe and its has a pleasant mild scent. Hardy to 0°F (−18°C), US zones 7–10.

Mentha × verticillata

Red Raripila
Mentha × smithiana 'Rubra' This has conspicuously deep red, tall strong stems and is thought to be a cross between Corn Mint, Water Mint and Spearmint. Whatever its parentage, it is an attractive plant almost totally resistant to rust which afflicts so many other mints. It requires plenty of room, as it eventually grows up to about 5ft (1.5m) tall, but will reward you with attractive, healthy looking green leaves with a spearmint scent, and whorls of small pale purple flowers distributed up the stem. The leaves are good in mint sauce, with young potatoes and peas and in long summer drinks such as Pimms. Hardy to 0°F (−18°C), US zones 7–10.

Red Raripila
Mentha × smithiana 'Rubra'

Peppermint *Mentha × piperita*

Black Peppermint *Mentha × piperita piperita*

Peppermint *Mentha × piperita* This hybrid between Water Mint and Spearmint is widely cultivated by amateurs and commercial growers in Europe, North and South America, Australia and parts of Asia. It grows to about 3ft (90cm) tall and has stalked, long, slightly hairy leaves with serrated edges, and bears spikes of lilac pink flowers in summer. Its familiar pungent smell and taste is valued as a flavouring in sweets, sorbets and puddings, and for making tea and liqueurs. Hardy to 0°F (–18°C), US zones 7–10.

Black Peppermint *Mentha × piperita piperita* A form of Peppermint which has deep purple upright stems to about 2ft (60cm) tall, and leaves tinged with purple. Commercial Peppermint oil is usually produced from this variety. Hardy to 0°F (–18°C), US zones 7–10.

Eau de Cologne Mint *Mentha × piperita* 'Citrata' A variety of Peppermint, this form grows to about 2ft (60cm) tall. It has smooth stalked, slightly bronze purplish green leaves that smell like Eau de Cologne, and small clusters of lilac purple flowers. It is invasive, sending out purple runners both below and above the ground. The aromatic qualities are most pronounced if this mint is grown in a sunny spot but it needs moisture, so be ready to water it during dry weather. The leaves can be added to cool drinks, fruit salads and herb jellies, but as the scent is better than its flavour, they are probably better dried and used in pot pourri. Hardy to 0°F (–18°C), US zones 7–10.

Eau de Cologne Mint *Mentha × piperita* 'Citrata'

MINT

Horsemint *Mentha longifolia*

Ginger Mint *Mentha × gracilis*

Curled or Curly Spearmint
Mentha spicata 'Crispa'
A decorative form of Spearmint that
has attractive pale green leaves with
curled edges. It grows up to 18in
(45cm) tall and bears small clusters
of pale lilac flowers at the top of
the stems during summer. It can
be used for the same purposes as
ordinary Spearmint as it smells
and tastes the same. The one
shown here was found in
Tashkent, Central Asia.
Hardy to −10°F (−23°C),
US zones 6–9.

Ginger or Scotch Mint
Mentha × gracilis formerly *Mentha ×
gentilis* A hybrid which has
Spearmint as one of its parents, this
mint is quite variable, but usually
grows to about 3ft (90cm) tall. Its
erect branched stems are often tinged
with red. The small green leaves
splashed with gold are pointed at each
end and attached to the main stems by

Curly
Spearmint
*Mentha
spicata*
'Crispa'

Spearmint *Mentha spicata*

short stalks. Unlike other mints, its lilac flowers are clustered up the main stem in the leaf axils, instead of being borne in spikes at the end of the stems. The leaves have a delicate flavour. Hardy to 0°F (–18°C), US zones 7–10.

Horsemint *Mentha longifolia*   Also known as Long-leaved Mint and Buddleia Mint because of its dense spikes of lilac (or sometimes white) flowers which look similar to those of Buddleia. It grows to about 2½ft (75cm) tall and has hairy stems with stalkless, woolly, slightly greyish leaves. There are also various hybridized forms between this and Spearmint which sometimes confuses the issue. Horsemint has a slightly musty scent and is not really one of the best mints for culinary use, but it is attractive to look at and can be used at a pinch. Hardy to 0°F (–18°C), US zones 7–10.

Spearmint *Mentha spicata*   Probably the most well-known and commonly grown of the mints, and justifiably so, for its leaves have a wonderfully fresh taste which combines well with many other ingredients. It grows to about 2½ft (75cm) tall and bears lilac pink flowers during summer and early autumn. This is the mint that is often used to make mint sauce or jelly to accompany lamb dishes; it is also used to flavour peas or boiled new potatoes, because it reaches its peak in the garden at just the right moment. Hardy to –10°F (–23°C), US zones 6–9.

Spearmint

Purple Sage leaves provide an attractive contrast to the foliage of strawberries and flowers of pansies

Purple Sage *Salvia officinalis* 'Purpurascens'

Common Sage *Salvia officinalis*

Sage

The sages are perennial herbs characterized by their aromatic leaves and distinctive hooded flowers. They have long been used in cooking, chiefly in stuffings for poultry and as a flavouring in sausages, but also in the cheeses known as 'Sage Derby' and 'Sage Lancashire'. Deborah Madison gives a good recipe for olive oil bread (*Focaccia*) with sage leaves, and another for a bean and tomato soup with sage and parsley. Some

'Icterina'

Turkish dishes (see Irfan Orga's book) such as *Cerkes Tavuga*, use small quantities of sage. Paul Bertolli gives a wonderful and unusual recipe for Pumpkin Tortelli with Brown Butter and Sage, accompanied by Sage Sauce. Sage also goes well with roast pork and at one time infusions were drunk as a remedy for colds and fevers. The flavour of sage is very strong and should be used sparingly. Leaves for drying are best harvested before flowering; dry them slowly and then crumble into airtight jars. Sages are found in the wild throughout southern Europe, parts of Asia and North Africa and are widely grown throughout Europe.

SAGE

'Icterina', a variegated form of sage

White Sage *Salvia officinalis* 'Albiflora'

PLANTING HELP Sages are native to warm dry areas, and therefore grow best in sunny, warm, sheltered places in good, well-drained soil. Despite this, most varieties here are reasonably hardy to 0°F (−18°C) provided they are not waterlogged. Sages can also be grown in containers and then taken indoors at the onset of cold weather.

The easiest way to propagate Common Sage is by layering. New plants can also be obtained by division or taking cuttings from young shoots on an established plant in late spring or early summer; these can be grown on in pots outside and replanted elsewhere. All sages benefit from trimming back immediately after flowering, which will keep the bush in good shape, but after five or six years the plant will normally need replacing as it will have become leggy and woody by then.

Common or **Garden Sage** *Salvia officinalis*
This shrub is native to the Mediterranean and North Africa, and likes a warm sunny place in the garden. It is also surprisingly hardy, needing protection only in prolonged periods of very severe cold. It grows to about 2ft (60cm) tall and wide, and develops a woody stem from which smaller branches arise bearing the fresh young leaves used for cooking. The thick furry leaves are narrowly oblong and greyish green; the flowers are a mauvy purple. There is a broad-leaved variant, *S. officinalis* 'Latifolia' (*not illustrated*) which is often sold specifically for culinary use; it flowers very rarely, with the result that young leaves are produced for a longer period. Hardy to 0°F (−18°C), US zones 7–10.

There are numerous other cultivars of Common Sage including:

'Icterina' (also known as Golden Sage or Variegated Sage) which has light green and golden variegated leaves, and makes an attractive, neat little bush up to about 16in (40cm) tall. Its mildly flavoured leaves are as good as, or better than Common Sage. Hardy to 0°F (−18°C), US zones 7–10; in our garden it has just weathered ten consecutive days when the temperature never rose above freezing.

Purple Sage *Salvia officinalis* 'Purpurascens' This variety grows up to 2ft (60cm) tall and wide with purple leaves and bluish mauve flowers. There is also a variegated form (*not illustrated here*). Hardy to 0°F (−18°C), US zones 7–10.

White Sage *Salvia officinalis* 'Albiflora' As the name implies, this attractive and less common variety has white flowers and much longer greener leaves than the common type. Hardy to 0°F (−18°C), US zones 7–10.

Common Sage

SAGE

Clary Sage *Salvia sclarea*

Clary Sage

Clary Sage *Salvia sclarea* Clary was a herb of some importance in the past and was included by William Turner in *A new herball* in 1551. The flowers were commonly used to flavour beer and wine while the leaves were sometimes used in fritters and other desserts. An essential oil commonly used in aromatherapy is extracted from the flowering tops and leaves.

Clary is native to S Europe and Asia where it grows in dry rocky places. It is a short-lived perennial, easily grown from seed, which produces flowering stems up to 3½ft (1m) tall in the summer of its second year, making a dramatic feature in the garden. The bracts are white, pink or pale mauve. Very hardy to –10°F (–23°C), US zones 6–9.

Meadow Clary *Salvia pratensis* This attractive form has larger flowers than Clary Sage, and was used by German wine merchants as a flavouring for muscatel wine – hence its common German name *Muskateller Salbei* (Muscatel Sage). Carter, in his herbal of 1736, gives a recipe for Clary Wine, and it was also commonly used to add flavour to ale. It is native to most of Europe, as far north as England where it is now very rare, and Russia, where it grows in fields and waste places. It has erect stems, and can grow up to 3½ft (1m) tall, though usually grows to about 2ft (60cm) tall. The violet blue flowers appear during early summer and are followed by seeds which were formerly used to improve and clear eyesight, hence the name 'Clary', from the Latin *clarus*, 'to clear'. Meadow Clary will tolerate rather damper conditions than some of the other sages, although it still prefers well-drained soil; add a little chalk before planting to improve its growth. Hardy to −10°F (−23°C), US zones 6–9.

Painted Sage *Salvia viridis* (syn. *S. horminum*)
When John Tradescant, gardener to Charles I, published his *Catalogue* in 1656 which listed the plants he grew in his garden at Lambeth, he included six *Salvias*, one of which was Painted Sage. Since that time, the Latin name has changed at least twice, but the common name survives, although it is often confused with True Clary *(Salvia sclarea)*. This is a strange plant with pink- or purple-coloured bracts, and it is usually grown as an annual or biennial bush from seed. Native to the Mediterranean region, it appreciates a warm sunny spot, where it will reward you by growing up to 18in (45cm) tall. There are several forms of this species, with bracts ranging from white through pink and blue to purple; the cultivar illustrated here is 'Bluebeard'. In the past, the leaves were used for flavouring drinks and a modern use for it is as an addition to Pimms. Hardy to −10°F (−23°C), US zones 6–9.

Pineapple Sage *Salvia rutilans*
possibly a form of *Salvia elegans*
This species has a most unusual scent of pineapple. It is also very attractive with bright red flowers, but is rather tender since it is native to Mexico. Unless you happen to live in a warm sunny climate, it is best treated as a conservatory plant. It may be grown in a pot and plunged outside in a bed during the summer, but it must be brought inside as soon as the nights start to get cold. This sage usually makes a substantial plant, up to 3ft (90cm) tall and about 2ft (60cm) wide. The green leaves are slightly tinged with red, and are good in fruit salads or sponge cakes. Hardy to 32°F (0°C), US zone 10.

Meadow Clary *Salvia pratensis*

Painted Sage
Salvia viridis

Pineapple Sage *Salvia rutilans*

Lavender

Although we said earlier that only those herbs of proven culinary use would be included, we have stretched a point here, simply because lavenders are one of our favourite groups of plants, and have traditionally been planted in the herb garden, often as edging plants for low hedges. In fact, lavender has been much used for medicinal and soothing purposes, and many people claim that lavender oil is a wonderful cure for headaches and insomnia.

To be honest, it is hard to find many culinary uses for lavender, except in peripheral things such as lavender jelly and tea, and crystallized flowers for use in cake decoration. This is the case because the smell is so particularly overpowering (and delicious) that it needs to be used in very small quantities. A few brave souls, however, have made an effort. At The Inn, a highly rated small restaurant in Little Washington, USA, they serve lavender-scented crème brûlée, while Norfolk Lavender in England sells lavender-scented tea and lavender-flavoured marmalade. Bees love lavender and the late-flowering varieties, such as 'Grappenhall', are particularly useful to them; honey from hives kept in lavender fields is prized for its good flavour.

There are 28 different species of lavender from the Mediterranean, North Africa, Arabia and India, and numerous named cultivated varieties. They are all aromatic shrubs of varying degrees of hardiness, some of the least tender being English

Lavender 'Hidcote'

Lavender *Lavandula angustifolia*, which has long been grown in Britain, and some of the cultivars which are derived from it.

PLANTING HELP All lavenders grow naturally in exposed, usually dry and hot rocky places, therefore lavender requires well-drained soil in cultivation. The actual soil type is not important, but avoid waterlogging, especially during the winter months. Lavenders can be grown from seed, but are usually propagated by cuttings taken from new growth in early summer or from the shoots after flowering at the end of summer. A number of specialist lavender growers now offer 'plugs', or rooted cuttings. Some of the English lavenders and the related hardy cultivars *L. latifolia* and *L. × intermedia*, become untidy after a few years and will need to be replaced by new plants. To keep your plants as long as possible, trim back in spring (taking cuttings at the same time if required), dead-head after flowering and trim back as hard as you can in early autumn, but avoid cutting into the old wood.

If you are growing varieties that are tender in your part of the world, take steps to protect the plants from extreme cold and wet by covering with fleece or bringing indoors, if in containers. Plants should be well watered-in when first planted; after that water sparingly during the summer and not at all in the winter. If grown in containers, a regular feed of liquid fertilizer during the growing season will help to promote flowering.

Common or **English Lavender** *Lavandula angustifolia* This hardy evergreen is native to the Mediterranean region, but is one of the hardiest species, making it popular with gardeners in temperate climates. When mature, the bush is

'Papillon', a fine form of the French Lavender *Lavandula stoechas*

Lavandula stoechas 'Alba'

LAVENDER

Lavender 'Grappenhall' at Quince House, Devon

about 3½ft (1m) tall and wide. The long narrow leaves are grey green and very aromatic; it is covered with spikes of fragrant purplish blue flowers. Hardy to 0°F (−18°C), US zones 7–10. There are several varieties of English Lavender, including two quite common white varieties, *Lavandula angustifolia* 'Alba' and *L. angustifolia* 'Nana Alba' which is a dwarf variety (*not illustrated*). Possibly the two most well-known garden varieties are:

'Hidcote' One of the best-known lavenders, this variety is often used for low hedges or edges as it makes a compact plant to about 16in (40cm) and produces its dark blue flowers freely throughout the summer. Hardy to 0°F (−18°C), US zones 7–10.

'Munstead' Another hardy variety very suitable for hedging, as it is low-growing to about 18in (45cm) and bears its purplish blue flowers on short stems. Hardy to 0°F (−18°C), US zones 7–10.

French Lavender *Lavandula stoechas* This attractive and aromatic evergreen

shrub is native to Spain and Portugal and is commonly grown throughout the Mediterranean region. It grows up to about 20in (50cm) tall and bears small dark mauve flowers on a short-stalked spike in early summer. It is of slightly doubtful hardiness in parts of Britain and N Europe, but will tolerate temperatures down to about 10°F (−12°C), US zones 8–10. However, it hates being waterlogged, so try to provide a really well-drained soil, and if you live in N Europe put it in the sunniest part of your garden. **Lavandula stoechas 'Alba'** is a low-growing white form.

'Grappenhall' *Lavandula × intermedia* 'Grappenhall' This is a good variety for low hedging as it soon bulks up into a decent dense bush, up to about 2½ft (75cm) tall after two or three years. The leaves are aromatic and greenish grey, and soft lilac blue flowers are borne late in the summer, persisting through the early autumn, on stems which rise about 12in (30cm) above the leaves. Hardy to 0°F (−18°C), US zones 7–10.

English Lavender

Lavender 'Munstead'

Rosemary 'Corsican Blue'

Rosemary

Rosemary is one of the most delightful of the shrubby herbs. Its strong scent evokes happy memories of summer trips to warm places abroad, and even in the mists of an English autumn its lingering fragrance is surprisingly pronounced. Rosemary has been used for culinary purposes since early times and it is often used with meat, particularly lamb, with which it seems to have a special affinity. It also blends well with fish and tomato dishes, and can be used to flavour herb jellies, olive oils and vinegars. There is a recipe for rosemary pasta in *The Greens Cookbook* which you could try if you like to make your own pasta, and the same book has a recipe for olive oil bread (*Focaccia)* with

Rosmarinus officinalis

rosemary. Some people object to eating the rather tough leaves, and my way round the problem is to infuse the leaves in a little warm water and add the liquid, rather than a branch of rosemary, to the dish. In his *Herball* Gerard makes extravagant claims for the flowers, saying that "The floures made up into plates with sugar after the manner of the Sugar Roset and eaten, comfort the heart, and make it merry, quicken the spirits, and make them more lively".

It is not really necessary to grow many different varieties since they all taste more or less the same. But they have different habits of growth and are suited to different areas of the garden; some will hang over walls while others make upright shrubs which can be used for hedging. As rosemary is truly evergreen there seems little point in drying it, unless you wish to give it away to other people, in which case it can be dried satisfactorily in the normal way.

PLANTING HELP   Rosemary requires a sunny well-drained soil to thrive. If these conditions are provided it will withstand quite low

Rosmarinus officinalis

Rosemary 'Fota Blue'

temperatures 10°F (–12°C), US zones 8–10, although if really cold weather is on the way you should provide some protection by covering with straw or fleece. Note that the prostrate varieties are less hardy. As with lavenders, waterlogging must be avoided and if your garden soil is unsuitable it would be better to grow the plants in containers and to bring them under cover for the winter. Incidentally, for those with seaside gardens, it should be noted that rosemaries are happy in a maritime climate and will withstand a considerable amount of salt spray.

If your plants need trimming back, do this after the first flush of flowering in spring, not in autumn, although some rosemaries seem virtually never to stop flowering! Rosemaries can be sown from seed, but it is much easier to grow them from cuttings; it is also the only way of being sure of the variety. Take 4in (10cm) cuttings in late summer from non-flowering shoots and if you like, dip them in rooting hormone mixture to help them along. Remove the lowest leaves and push them into a tray of good compost mixture; keep in a frost-free place until the following spring when they can be hardened off and planted out. Remember that after a couple of years most

rosemaries will make quite large (or spreading) bushes, so do not plant too closely.

Rosmarinus officinalis The better known of the two species that exist, it is quite variable and has given rise to many named cultivars, some of which are listed below. In the wild *Rosmarinus officinalis* is an evergreen shrub that grows up to 7ft (2m) in favourable conditions, with narrow aromatic, green leaves borne on upright branches, and flowers varying in colour from pale blue through to dark blue and occasionally appearing pink or white. Hardy to 10°F (–12°C), US zones 8–10, depending on conditions. Of the many varieties available we illustrate the following:

'Corsican Blue' Another beautiful but slightly tender creeping variety from Corsica with deep blue flowers. Hardy (for short periods only) to 20°F (–6°C), US zones 9–10.

'Fota Blue' A low-growing but fairly hardy form with narrow dark green leaves and dark blue flowers which appear from early spring onwards. Hardy to 10°F (–12°C), US zones 8–10, depending on conditions.

ROSEMARY

Prostrate
Rosemary

Rosemary 'Miss
Jessup's Upright'

Rosemary 'Miss Jessup's Upright'
(syn. 'Fastigiatus') One of the hardier upright
varieties of rosemary with broad leaves and pale
blue flowers. Good for hedging as it can make a
dense bush up to 7ft (2m) high in good
conditions. Hardy to 10°F (−12°C), US zones
8–10, depending on conditions.

Rosemary 'Roseus' A very
good highly aromatic, pink-
flowered variety, similar in habit
to 'Miss Jessup's Upright', which
has done well on a stony south-
facing bank in our garden in
north Devon. Despite 'scorching'
of the shoot tips by frost, this
bush has grown up to about 3½ft
(1m) and has flowered more or
less continuously throughout the
year. There is another pink form
sold under the name 'Majorca
Pink' which flowers early in the
New Year (*not illustrated here*).
Hardy (for short periods only) to
20°F (−6°C), US zones 9–10.

Rosemary 'Benenden Blue' A semi-prostrate
slightly tender, narrow-leaved form with bright
blue flowers, introduced to Britain from Corsica
by Collingwood (Cherry) Ingram and named after
his garden at Benenden in Kent. Hardy (for short
periods only) to 20°F (−6°C), US zones 9–10, but
should be given a sheltered position in the garden.

Prostrate or Prostratus Group (syns. *Rosmarinus
repens*, *Rosmarinus lavandulaceus*) A term used to
describe a group of trailing varieties with light
blue flowers. Less hardy than the *R. officinalis*
varieties, these will tolerate strong salt-laden
winds, but are unlikely to survive temperatures
below 20°F (−6°C), US zones 9–10. They do well
in California and Bermuda.

Rosemary 'Sissinghurst Blue'
A densely growing upright variety
with medium blue flowers in late
spring and early summer, this can
make a plant up to about 5ft (1.5m).
This originated as a self-sown
seedling in Vita Sackville-West's
garden at Sissinghurst, Kent.
Hardy to 10°F (−12°C), US
zones 8–10, depending on
conditions.

Rosemary 'Roseus'

Rosemary 'Benenden Blue'

Rosemary 'Sissinghurst Blue'

Rosemary 'Tuscan Blue' A very good upright variety with broader, bright green leaves that have a white underside and large bright blue flowers. It is used for hedges in Tuscany, from whence it was brought to Britain. Rather tender and it needs trimming back if you want plenty of flowers. Hardy (for short periods only) to 20°F (–6°C), US zones 9–10.

Hyssop

Hyssop is related to savory and is a most attractive plant worth growing for its looks alone; it is also useful in the kitchen. There are about 10 different species native to S Europe east to Central Asia, but the one commonly used for cooking is Blue Hyssop (*Hyssopus officinalis*) and its various forms.

It has been valued chiefly as a medicinal herb, mainly to treat respiratory problems, but the strong peppery taste of the leaves is also good when used in stuffing for roast meat or in thick soups or stews. It is used in the making of some types of liqueur and goes well with some types of fruit (for example, to flavour fruit pies in the US). Both leaves and flowers can be dried and used as part of a bouquet garni. **NB**: Do not eat hyssop during pregnancy, as it can occasionally cause muscle spasms.

PLANTING HELP   Hyssop likes a good well-drained soil and a warm sunny position. It dislikes waterlogged conditions, but will tolerate quite cold weather and is hardy to 20°F (–6°C), US zones 9–10. Protection in the form of cloches, fleece, bracken or straw should be provided if temperatures drop much below this.

Hyssop can be grown outside as a pot plant or as an attractive low hedge. It can be raised from seed sown in moist soil in spring or from cuttings of young growth taken in late spring or early summer. If grown from seed, pot on the seedlings and gradually harden off before planting out at intervals of about 12in (30cm).

Hyssop or **Blue Hyssop** *Hyssopus officinalis*
A perennial from S and E Europe which has also become naturalised in other parts of Europe and the US. It can become quite large in good conditions, but is usually about 2ft (60cm) tall and wide. Narrow aromatic leaves, and small deep blue flowers are carried on a narrow spike in late summer. A variable species, there are different colour forms including: **Pink Hyssop** (*H. officinalis* 'Roseus') and **White Hyssop** (*H. officinalis* 'Albus'). There is a subspecies, **Rock Hyssop** (*H. officinalis aristatus*), which is smaller, 12in (30cm) and has darker blue flowers. Hardy to 20°F (–6°C), US zones 9–10.

Rosemary 'Tuscan Blue'

Blue and White Hyssop

Pink Hyssop *Hyssopus officinalis* 'Roseus'

Rock Hyssop *Hyssopus officinalis aristatus*

Savory

There are 30 species of savory, mostly native to Europe and SW Asia, but the two commonly used in cooking are Winter Savory and Summer Savory. Two other savories available commercially that can be used for cooking are Broadleaf Savory and Creeping Savory; all four savories have fragrant foliage and small flowers which are attractive to bees.

Because of the strong volatile oil it contains, savory has a long history of domestic use, being considered useful both as a flavouring and as an aid to digestion – attributes that have lead to its common use in dishes such as the bean soups of Italy and France where it is sometimes called the

Broadleaf Savory
Satureja thymbria

'bean herb'. In France it is known as *sarriette*, and the leaves are used to flavour dishes of broad or haricot beans. Savory is also an ingredient of some types of salami and is occasionally used with other meats.

PLANTING HELP Both Summer and Winter Savory can be grown from seed. As the seeds are minute, it is easier to grow small quantities indoors, although it can be sown *in situ* once the soil has warmed up. If sowing indoors, provide plenty of light to help germination, a process which can take weeks, and pot on once the seedlings are large enough to handle. Whereas Summer Savory is an annual and seed must be sown each year, Winter Savory is a perennial, hardy to about 10°F (−12°C), US zones 8–10, and can be kept for many years. Cut it back to the woody base each spring and protect it from extreme cold, either by covering or by digging it up and bringing indoors where it can be grown as a pot plant. Winter Savory can also be grown from cuttings taken with a woody heel. All savories like good well-drained soil and a hot dry sunny position; if pot-grown, they need a good free-draining compost. Summer Savory prefers slightly alkaline conditions. Make sure that the plants never become waterlogged – the combination of too much water and severe cold will kill them. This does not mean that they never need watering, however, so water sparingly during hot weather.

Broadleaf Savory *Satureja thymbria* This lesser known but very attractive little shrub is native to the Balkans. It grows to around 12in (30cm) tall. Small pale pink flowers are borne in whorls up the stem during early summer. Best treated as an annual in cool areas as it is not very hardy; it will probably withstand temperatures down to 32°F (0°C), US zone 10.

Creeping Savory *Satureja spicigera* (syn. *Satureja reptans*) A creeping perennial native to SW Asia, with small narrow leaves and little white flowers which appear during late summer. This savory does best in well-drained soil in a hot dry sunny place in the garden or can be grown satisfactorily in a pot. Hardy to 0°F (-18°C), US zones 7–10.

Summer Savory *Satureja hortensis* An aromatic shrubby annual native to SE Europe, which grows up to about 12in (30cm). It has small narrow leaves and little clusters of small purplish white flowers. The first leaves will normally be ready for use in about June, and by nipping out the flowers and the young shoots for use in cooking, you will help to keep the bush in good shape. The leaves dry well. Hardy to 10°F (−12°C), US zones 8–10.

Summer Savory *Satureja hortensis*

Creeping Savory *Satureja spicigera*

Winter Savory *Satureja montana*

Winter Savory *Satureja montana*   Native to S Europe, this attractive little woody perennial bush grows up to 12in (30cm) tall. It has been grown for many years as a pot-herb and is sometimes found naturalized in Britain and N Europe. It has small, narrow, dark green leaves and tiny purple white flowers that appear up the stem in the leaf axils in the summer. The flavour is stronger than Summer Savory, so use sparingly. It is useful in late autumn once Summer Savory is gone. Its affinity with red meat makes it a useful herb to have as the weather starts to get colder and appetites long for heartier, heavier winter fare. Hardy to 10°F (−12°C), US zones 8–10.

Variegated Lemon Balm *Melissa officinalis* 'Aurea'

Variegated Lemon Balm

Lemon Balm in flower

Golden Lemon Balm *Melissa officinalis* 'All Gold'

Lemon Balm

The name Bee Balm (*melissa* is the Greek for 'honeybee') stems from the fact that bees are attracted to the flowers and produce good honey from the nectar. Gerard, in his *Herball* published in 1636, describes Melissa as 'our common best known balme or Bawme...drawing neere in smell and savour unto a Citron'. He then goes on to list the extraordinary uses to which it might be put, including drinking the leaves with wine as a cure 'against the stingings of venomous beasts, and the biting of mad dogs', and so on. Interestingly, he nowhere suggests that it should be used simply for its pleasant taste! The lemon-flavoured leaves are best used when young, and are good in stuffings, seasonings and sauces, as well as in summer drinks. It makes a very refreshing tea – we just put

Lemon Balm *Melissa officinalis*

a handful of young leaves into a teapot, pour over boiling water and leave to infuse for a few minutes. The leaves can be dried, but they seem to lose most of their taste.

PLANTING HELP   Lemon Balm grows well in almost any soil, in sun or shade, although it prefers a dry well-drained site, and is actually quite drought-resistant. It can be very invasive as it spreads by means of a creeping woody rootstock, so thought should be given to restraining it before it takes over. If using in the kitchen, keep trimming back the shoots to ensure a continuous supply of fresh young leaves. Propagate by taking cuttings of young shoots in early summer, by division or by sowing seeds in the spring (the coloured leaf varieties will not come true from seed).

Lemon Balm or **Bee Balm** *Melissa officinalis*
A perennial bush native to S Europe and found naturalized in parts of Britain, it grows up to 3ft (90cm) tall and produces small whitish yellow flowers during summer and early autumn. Hardy to 0°F (−18° C), US zones 7–10.

Golden Lemon Balm *Melissa officinalis* 'All Gold'   This has completely golden leaves and benefits from some shade; cut it back after flowering to maintain the golden colour. Hardy to 0°F (−18°C), US zones 7–10.

Variegated Lemon Balm *Melissa officinalis* 'Aurea'   This has green leaves splashed with cream that can be used in the same way as ordinary Lemon Balm. The disadvantage of this one is that it seeds itself very freely, and the seedlings frequently revert to the original (green) form. This is why it needs to be propagated from cuttings. Hardy to 0°F (−18°C), US zones 7–10.

Lemon Balm

Bergamot *Monarda didyma* 'Melissa'

Bergamot *Monarda didyma*

Bergamot

Bergamot is native to North America, there are 16 species. The most commonly grown in herb gardens is *Monarda didyma*. The young leaves and flowers are edible and can be mixed into salads. The leaves yield oil of bergamot, and can also be used (fresh or dried) to make a herbal tea – a drink that was popular with the North American Oswego Indians. Referred to as Bee Balm because it attracts bees, and as Bergamot because of the similarity of its scent to that of Bergamot Orange.

Monarda didyma 'Beauty of Cobham'

PLANTING HELP Bergamot makes a good bushy plant and and is often grown in herbaceous borders and in herb gardens, although it takes up a lot of room when fully grown. It needs rich, moist soil in sun or partial shade and is invasive.

Propagate by dividing the plants every two or three years, throwing away the old roots and replanting the young ones where required. Bergamot species can also be grown from seed sown under glass in spring, but the cultivars will not come true from seed. Take cuttings from all types in early summer. Wild Bergamot, a native of Mexico and N America, will tolerate drier conditions, so if you have poor, well-drained soil you might try this variety or one of the cultivars of *M. didyma*. Most bergamots (especially the species) are prone to mildew which attacks the base of the plant if it becomes too dry; if you spot signs of greying leaves, cut the whole plant back down to the base.

Bergamot, Bee Balm or **Oswego Tea** *Monarda didyma* This highly scented perennial herb grows in rich woodland soil and by streams, and can reach up to 5ft (1.5m) tall, although it is more usually about 3ft (90cm) tall. The rough-toothed dark green leaves grow in pairs up the stems, at the top of which curiously shaped red flowers bloom during summer. It is hardy to about –10°F (–23°C), US zones 6–9. The original species is most usually grown for culinary use, but there are numerous cultivars of *M. didyma* that can also be

Monarda didyma 'Cambridge Scarlet'

Monarda didyma 'Croftway Pink'

Wild Bergamot *Monarda fistulosa*

planted to add variety; these are generally more tolerant of dry conditions than *M. didyma*.

'Beauty of Cobham'   Has pale pink flowers and purplish foliage. Hardy to about −10°F (−23°C), US zones 6–9.

'Cambridge Scarlet'   This is a very popular and widely available form with dark red flowers. Often used in herbaceous borders. It grows to about 3ft (90cm) tall. Hardy to about −10°F (−23°C), US zones 6–9.

'Croftway Pink'   An attractive variety which grows to about 3ft (90cm) tall.

'Melissa'   Rather a doubtful name, but a pretty

plant. The photograph shows how attractive a good clump can look when planted in with other large perennials. Hardy to about −10°F (−23°C), US zones 6–9.

Wild Bergamot *Monarda fistulosa*   In the wild this species grows in dry scrub and on the edges of woods, and in the garden it does well in any good soil in sun or partial shade. It has greyish stalkless leaves and lilac, pink or whitish flowers, and grows to about 5ft (1.5m) tall. The leaves and flowers can both be used sparingly in salads. Hardy to about −20°F (−29°C), US zones 5–9.

Perilla frutescens 'Atropurpurea'

Japanese Perilla *Perilla frutescens*

Perilla

This group of
about six species of
annual herbs is native
to India and China where it
grows in the mountains. The
most commonly grown in
gardens is *Perilla frutescens*, a
very popular herb in Japan
where it is much used as a garnish and to flavour
fish, bean curd, tempura dishes and pickle. It is
also cultivated both in China and Japan for the
aromatic oil which is extracted from the seeds.

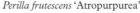

Perilla frutescens
var. *nankinensis*

PLANTING HELP   Perillas prefer full sun in
good, slightly acid, moist soil, but will not tolerate
waterlogging. They are best propagated from seed
sown under glass in spring; these germinate easily
and the seedlings can be planted out once the soil
has warmed up.

Japanese or **Common Perilla** *Perilla frutescens*
A hairy annual that grows up to 3½ft (1m) tall. It
has broad, deeply serrated, aromatic green leaves
that are sometimes blotched with purple, and its

white flowers appear in summer. Hardy to 10°F
(−12°C), US zones 8–10.
'Atropurpurea' (syn. *Perilla* f. *rubra*)   A form
with dark reddish purple leaves. We have seen
plastic purple perilla used in Japanese lunchboxes!
Hardy to 10°F (−12°C), US zones 8–10.

Perilla frutescens* var. *nankinensis (syns.
'Crispa', 'Aka Shiso')   This is a cultivated form
from China which has distinctive curled purple
leaves. These purple forms are used for
ornamental purposes as well as for culinary use,
and in the past could be seen growing in bedding
schemes in municipal public parks in Britain.
Hardy to 10°F (−12°C), US zones 8–10.

Agastache

Although there are 20 species of the so-called
Giant or Mexican Hyssops, we have illustrated
only two of the hardier ones (*see opposite*) which
are normally grown for culinary use. Aromatic
perennials native to North America, China and
Japan, they are quite commonly used in the US,
although they are not so widely grown in Britain
and N Europe at present.

AGASTACHE

Anise Hyssop *Agastache foeniculum* in the herb garden at Arley Hall

PLANTING HELP   Both Anise Hyssop and Korean Mint need a sheltered well-drained position in good soil, preferably in full sun. Both species can be grown in large containers outside, provided that they are not allowed to dry out. Anise Hyssop is hardy to 10°F (−12°C), US zones 8–10 provided it is not waterlogged; during cold spells it is wise to protect both this and Korean Mint (which is slightly less hardy) with fleece. Both can be grown from seed or cuttings taken in spring or late summer, or the plants can be divided and replanted in early spring.

Anise Hyssop *Agastache foeniculum*, (syn. *Agastache anethiodora*)   An upright-growing perennial native to C North America, but naturalized in New England where it grows in fields, dry scrub and in the hills. A bushy plant that grows up to about 3½ft (1m) tall, it has ovate, strongly aniseed-scented green leaves tinged with purple above and whitish underneath. Long spikes of violet purple flowers appear in summer and these are very attractive to bees. Anise Hyssop, sometimes known as Liquorice Mint, is popular in the US where the dried leaves are used to make a tea and young leaves are used in salads and summer drinks and as seasoning in savoury dishes. Hardy to 10°F (−12°C), US zones 8–10.

Korean Mint *Agastache rugosa*   A perennial plant native to China and Japan, growing to 3½ft (1m) tall, which is similar to Anise Hyssop, but with leaves that smell and taste of mint rather than aniseed. Like Anise Hyssop, it is attractive to bees and can be used to make a refreshing tea and to flavour salads and other dishes instead of mint. Hardy to 20°F (−6°C), US zones 9–10.

Korean Mint
Agastache rugosa

Oregano

There is general confusion over the names Oregano and Marjoram, which has arisen chiefly because the Latin name for Wild Marjoram or Oregano is *Origanum vulgare*. On these two pages we illustrate only this wild form and cultivars derived from it, and on the following two pages are some of the other species of *Origanum* which are commonly grown for their decorative features, but can also be used in the kitchen.

Oregano
Origanum vulgare

It is widely used throughout Europe in sausages, soups, stews, sauces and tomato recipes; in France and Italy (where it is an important ingredient of Pizza Napolitana) the leaves are used, whereas in Greece the dried flower heads (which keep their flavour well) are preferred and are used to flavour lamb kebabs.

Oregano has a long history of cultivation by the ancient Greeks and the Romans, and is wild on limestone in Britain where it has been used since medieval times. Tradescant listed five varieties of what he called 'Majorana' in 1656 and also included under the heading 'Origanum', 'the true Spanish Marjoram'.

Wild Marjoram or **Oregano** *Origanum vulgare*
A woody perennial herb native to most of Europe, including Britain where it grows on limestone hills and chalk downland, and to Asia as far east as Taiwan. It was a surprise to see this species growing wild on limestone hills in western Yunnan, the only English flowers among alien vegetation. This is a very variable species, but normally has stems 2ft (60cm) or more tall, and bears pinkish purple flowers throughout late summer. Other varieties have pink flowers, **'Roseum'**, or white, var. *album*, and there is the Golden Marjoram **'Aureum'**, and the dwarf **'Compactum'**. All the named varieties shown here are very hardy, down to 0°F (−18°C), US zones 7–10. They are good general garden plants, much loved by butterflies and bees. There has been much confusion in herb books and in nurseries, between the different forms of Oregano *Origanum vulgare*, and two quite different herbs called Sweet Marjoram *Origanum majorana* (also called Annual or Knotted Marjoram), and the closely related Pot or French Marjoram *Origanum onites*. Both these are southern European species, not hardy in Britain, northern Europe or Eastern

Wild Marjoram growing on the North Downs

Origanum vulgare 'Compactum'

Origanum vulgare 'Roseum'

Golden Marjoram in the herb garden at Ballymaloe Cookery School near Cork in Ireland

North America, surviving only 20°F (–6°C) US zones 9–10. Most plants bought as Pot Marjoram turn out to be forms of oregano. The three are not easy to distinguish with certainty unless they are flowering. In flower *Origanum vulgare* has a calyx with 5 teeth, while both *Origanum majorana* and *Origanum onites* have only a single-lipped calyx, deeply cleft along one side. The last two have pale flowers in tight little grey balls. *O. majorana* and *O. onites* are very similar to one another; *majorana* has small ball-like flower heads in an elongated arrangement on the flowering stems, *onites* has densely hairy stems, toothed leaves and a flat-topped arrangement of flower heads. Both have a sweeter, softer scent than oregano.

PLANTING HELP   All *Origanums* like well-drained, dry soil in full sun. Some, such as *Origanum calcaratum*, will do well planted in the crevice of a wall and most of the others will do best in a raised bed. Wild Marjoram (*Origanum vulgare*) and Sweet Marjoram (*Origanum marjorana*) can be grown from seed, which should be sown thinly as the seed is very fine, in spring, preferably with some bottom heat and kept only slightly moist. Pot on once the seedlings are big enought to handle. Put them out once the weather

is warm enough, growing them either in pots or in beds. The other forms shown here need to be propagated by cuttings or by division.

Most types are reasonably hardy, as long as they do not become waterlogged; the exception to this is *Origanum marjorana* which will only survive temperatures below freezing for very short periods. One way around this problem is to pot up one or two of each variety and bring them into the kitchen. If your outdoor plants succumb, you will be able to divide your indoor plants and replace them.

Oregano at a good stage for eating

Origanum rotundifolium

Origanum

Shown here are some of the other species and varieties that are available; all are aromatic and can be used for cooking in the same way as oregano. Dry by hanging in loose bunches in a warm well-ventilated place, then store in jars to be used in cooking, or use the bunches in arrangements of dried flowers, or in pot pourri.

PLANTING HELP   All the *Origanums* on this page prefer well-drained dry soil in full sun. Some, such as *Origanum calcaratum*, will do well planted in the crevice of a wall and most of the others will do best in a raised bed.

Origanum calcaratum (syn. *Origanum tournefortii*)   Native to Crete and other Aegean islands, this grows on limestone rocks (hence the name) up to about 12in (30cm) tall from a woody base, sending up many stems which bear greyish ovate leaves and pink bracts. It is easy to grow in Britain and N Europe, provided it does not become waterlogged. Take preventive action by covering the plant with a sheet of glass or a cloche during wet winter weather. Hardy to about 10°F (−12°C), US zones 8–10.

Origanum rotundifolium   An attractive species with round bluish leaves and round hop-like heads of pale green bracts almost hiding the whitish flowers. It is easily grown, but prefers moist well-drained soil. It will do well growing out of a dry wall, its stems running about behind the wall and emerging between the stones. *O. rotundifolium* is native to the dry inner valleys of the mountains south of Trabzon in northern Turkey, where it grows out of damp crevices in cliffs. Hardy to about 10° (−12°C), US zones 8–10.

Origanum rotundifolium 'Kent Beauty'

ORIGANUM

'Barbara Tingey' This is a hybrid between *Origanum calcaratum* and *Origanum rotundifolium*. It has very attractive pink bracts and dries well. Hardy to about 10°F (−12°C), US zones 8–10

'Hopleys' This pink-flowered form is named after Hopleys Nurseries, whose owner, David Barker, introduced it in about 1980. Hardy to about 0°F (−18°C), US zones 7–10.

'Kent Beauty' This hybrid was raised in Kent in about 1978 and has semi-creeping stems, greyish leaves and pink bracts. Hardy to about 10°F (−12°C), US zones 8–10.

'Emma Stanley' A hybrid with smooth grey leaves and attractive pink bracts, this appeared in Roger Poulett's garden in Sussex in 1985. Hardy to about 10°F (−12°C), US zones 8–10.

'Barbara Tingey'

Origanum calcaratum

'Hopleys'

'Emma Stanley'

Russian Tarragon

French Tarragon *Artemisia dracunculus* var. *sativa*

Tarragon

One of the most useful and delicious of all the culinary herbs, tarragon is a large, untidy herbaceous perennial. There are two forms with similar appearances but quite different flavours: for culinary use the less hardy French form is preferred to the coarser Russian type. Tarragon may have been introduced into cultivation comparatively recently, although it was correctly described by Gerard in his *Herball* of 1636, as a 'sallade herbe'. Both types of tarragon like a warm, sunny position and deep, well-drained soil, although the French variety prefers a rather richer soil; neither type will tolerate being waterlogged.

French
Tarragon

French Tarragon *Artemisia dracunculus* var. *sativa*
This is of uncertain origin, but probably comes from SE Russia. It makes a much-branched plant up to about 3ft (90cm) or more, with narrow, dark green leaves up to 3in (8cm) long, and sprays of tiny yellow flowers in summer. Tarragon is a useful culinary herb, with a unique and distinctive flavour which has a great affinity with white fish and veal and chicken; it is popular in France where it is an essential ingredient of traditional recipes such as *sauce béarnaise*, Montpellier butter and *sauce verte* (Jane Grigson has a good recipe in her *Fish Book*) and it is also used in *fines herbes* mixtures. It is used in many new recipes; *The Greens Cook Book* suggests using equal amounts of chopped parsley and tarragon to accompany fresh pasta with tomatoes and cream. Tarragon is good as a flavouring for omelettes, salads, fish dishes and creamy soups. Make tarragon vinegar simply by adding sprigs of the herb to bottles of ordinary wine vinegar, and allowing it to steep in a cool, dark place. The leaves can be dried and stored in the usual way, but are better frozen during the summer.

PLANTING HELP   French Tarragon generally needs replacing about every 3–4 years. Tarragon only sets seed if it is grown in exceptionally warm conditions. To propagate, either pull up shoots which have already rooted and replant them; or take root cuttings, either in early spring or in autumn. Replant, either in the place where they are required, or in medium-sized pots, where they will thrive provided they are given well-drained compost and plenty of moisture. As French Tarragon is not reliably hardy in cool areas, it is usually wise to cut outdoor plants back to about 4in (10cm) in the autumn, keeping a few cuttings in a pot of compost indoors in case the original plant is killed. The indoor plants can then be hardened off in the spring and either planted out in beds, or transferred to larger pots for the summer. Protect French Tarragon from low temperatures by using fleece or straw. Hardy to 20°F (−6°C), US zones 9–10.

Russian Tarragon *Artemisia.dracunculus* var. *inodora*   Inferior to French Tarragon for culinary purposes, this plant can be used if that is all you have available. Native to N Russia it is hardier and more vigorous than French Tarragon, and will make a plant up to about 5ft (1.5m) tall.It has narrow green leaves and tiny yellow flowers, but has virtually no scent and a rather bitter flavour.Hardy to −40°F (−40°C), US zones 3–8.

Purslane

An annual native to many areas of Europe and Asia, *Portulaca oleracea* is now widely naturalized throughout the warmer regions of the world, where it is found growing wild in fields, on roadsides and by the sea. It is a sprawling plant, growing up to about 6in (15cm) tall with soft, thick stems and glossy succulent leaves. The bright yellow flowers appear during the summer.

Purslane has been cultivated for centuries as a salad and pot herb. Its leaves have a mild flavour and a crisp texture, and are a good source of iron. They can be eaten raw in salads or cooked as a vegetable. It has long been used in Indian, Middle Eastern and Greek cooking, where the young fleshy leaves are thought to be a delicacy. In the Middle East it is used in a salad called *fattoush*. It is also an essential ingredient for *Soupe bonne femme*, and Jane Grigson has a French recipe for purslane and green pea soup.

Interesting recent research by the French National Institute for Health and Medical Research, shows that Purslane is an extremely good source of Omega 3, the essential fatty acid needed for a healthy heart. It is much eaten in Crete, whose population has one of the lowest heart disease rates in the world.

The leaves are ready for harvesting about six weeks after sowing; frequent picking and removal of flower heads will ensure a good supply of leaves until the plant is cut down by frost in the autumn.

PLANTING HELP   Purslane can be grown easily from seed, sown *in situ*, at intervals from early summer onwards to ensure a continuous supply of fresh leaves. An earlier crop can be obtained by sowing indoors and planting out once all danger of frost has passed. It can also be propagated by cuttings or root division in mid-spring. It does best in a moisture-retaining, well-drained soil in a sunny but sheltered position. Purslane will require watering during long, hot dry spells. Hardy to about 20°F (−6°C), US zones 9–10 or less.

Tarragon in a pot of mixed herbs

Purslane *Portulaca oleracea*

Salad Burnet

A perennial herb native to Europe, parts of Asia and N Africa, it is found wild on the chalk downs of S England and is also naturalized in North America. *Sanguisorba minor* grows to about 1ft (30cm) tall, and produces crimson flowers throughout summer. Salad Burnet was commonly grown in medieval times because the leaves could be harvested throughout much of the winter, a time when greenstuff was scarce. The feathery leaves, which have a nutty, slightly cucumbery taste, are good in winter soups, casseroles and sauces, such as *Beurre Montpellier*, or, in summer, can be added to drinks and salads. Salad Burnet, known as *pimprenelle* in France, featured in the recipe for Napoleon's daily salad eaten during his exile on St Helena, in which green herbs were used to cheer up a diet of haricot beans.

PLANTING HELP Salad Burnet is best grown from seed, sown in spring or autumn; it will often seed itself and the seedlings can be dug up and replanted where they are required. It grows best in light, preferably chalky, well-drained soil, thriving in sun or shade. Remove the flower heads to ensure a continuous supply of fresh young leaves. Pick the leaves frequently to encourage new growth. It is very hardy and will survive low temperatures outside, but it can be potted up and brought indoors to be grown as a pot plant on a kitchen windowsill. Hardy to −20°F (−29°C), US zones 5–9.

Salad Burnet *Sanguisorba minor*

Sweet Cicely

Garden Myrrh *Myrrhis odorata* A vigorous perennial herb, originating from S Europe and found growing wild in much of Britain and S Scotland, where it is particularly attractive on river banks. It is one of the earliest herbs to appear in spring, making a large feathery bush up to about 6ft (1.8m) with hollow stems and aromatic, fern-like pale green leaves, which turn purplish in autumn. Clusters of white flowers appear during early summer, and these should be removed immediately if you wish to ensure a good harvest of leaves. The leaves can be picked throughout most of the year, apart from mid-winter when the plant dies down to the ground. It has been esteemed as a sweet culinary herb for many years, with all parts of the plant being edible. The leaves have a sweet taste with a slight flavour of anise, and can be used as a sugar substitute. They are particularly good in fruit pies, or added fresh to salads, or cooked and used to flavour soups and stews. The roots can be boiled and eaten as a cold salad dish when served with dressing, and the seeds can be used chopped in sweet dishes to add a slightly nutty flavour.

PLANTING HELP In favourable conditions Sweet Cicely will self-seed, sometimes too enthusiastically; you can avoid this by dead-heading most of the plants immediately after flowering, keeping just enough seed for your own sowing. It grows well from fresh seed sown in the autumn, as the low winter temperatures encourage germination, but it can also be grown from bought dried seed sown in spring. It can also be propagated by division in autumn, or by root cuttings in spring or autumn. It needs a deep, moisture-retentive soil and sun or part shade. It is very hardy, surviving temperatures down to about 10°F (−12°C), US zones 8–10.

Sweet Cicely *Myrrhis odorata*

Sweet Cicely growing along the banks of the River Don, Aberdeenshire, Scotland

Angelica *Angelica archangelica* on Chiswick Eyot on the River Thames

Angelica

Archangel *Angelica archangelica* A vigorous, but short-lived perennial, originating from Central and N Europe, as far north as the Arctic, and is naturalized in Britain and elsewhere. It makes a large plant, about 7 ft (2m) or so tall, with branching stems and large, light green, divided leaves. The tiny creamy or greenish white flowers are borne in rounded clusters up to 6in (15cm) across.

The crystallized stalks are used for flavouring and decorating cakes and pastries. Elizabeth David says that in the Nivernais district of France it is used in powdered form for flavouring a cream cheese tart. The young leaves can be used fresh in salads, or cooked with fruits such as rhubarb or gooseberry to alleviate the sourness. The stalks can be cut and peeled and used fresh as a vegetable; although strongly scented, they have little taste. The seeds are used commercially in the making of liqueurs, such as Benedictine and Chartreuse. Harvest the stems in spring and the leaves during the early summer, prior to flowering.

PLANTING HELP Angelica makes an attractive large plant so give it plenty of room and place it in a shady corner, in moist but well-drained soil, where it can remain undisturbed. Be prepared to water in dry weather. Once it has flowered and seeded it will die, so you should either remove the flowers before seeding or collect the ripe seed (which soon loses its viability) and sow it immediately (in good conditions, the plant will seed itself freely). Angelica is extremely hardy (as can be seen from its distribution in the wild) and can withstand temperatures as low as −30°F (−35°C), US zones 4–8.

Alexanders *Smyrnium olustratum* growing wild above Romney Marsh

Alexanders

Black Lovage *Smyrnium olustratum*   A biennial plant native to SW Europe and widely naturalized in Britain and other parts of Europe. It is generally found growing near the sea on cliffs, in hedgerows and on rough ground. It grows up to about 5ft (1.5m) and has a stout stem, which becomes hollow with age, and large dark green, divided leaves. The rounded clusters of greenish yellow flowers appear during late spring and early April, and these are followed by the small black fruits.

The celery-flavoured leaves, stalks and roots were formerly used in soups, stews and salads and remained popular in Britain until it was largely replaced by celery and other root vegetables. It is worth trying as a vegetable; simply cut the stems and leaf stalks in late spring (before flowering), peel and cut into small pieces and boil or steam for a few minutes until tender, then serve with plenty of melted butter and season with ground black pepper.

Alexanders *Smyrnium olustratum*

PLANTING HELP   The seed of Alexanders can be sown in autumn or spring, but have patience as germination can be very slow. It likes a rich, moisture-retentive but well-drained soil in a sunny position in the garden. If you want to eat the stems blanch them first by earthing them up for a couple of weeks in the early spring. Hardy to 10°F (−12°C), US zones 8–10.

Horseradish *Armoricia rusticana* is beautiful but invasive

A variegated form of horseradish

Horseradish

A perennial originating from SE Europe, *Armoricia rusticana* is found naturalized throughout Britain and other parts of Europe and North America. It grows to about 2ft (60cm) tall, with a thick tuft of large, rather coarse, dark green leaves, and in summer sends up flowering stems to about 3½ft (1m) tall, which bear small white flowers. The long forked roots are very tough and where the plant escapes and is not wanted, it can be difficult to eliminate, as even small pieces of root will continue to grow. The root has a pungent taste and can be grated and used raw to make a creamy horseradish sauce, which goes well with roast beef or oily fish, such as smoked mackerel. The roots are best harvested in the second (or subsequent) autumn after planting. They can be stored in a tub of moist sand until needed, and the side shoots can be used for replanting in the spring to continue the crop.

PLANTING HELP   Horseradish grows easily from small pieces of root which should be planted

Lovage makes a stately plant in a walled garden   Lovage *Levisticum officinale*

about 1ft (30cm) apart in early spring, and are best left undisturbed for the first year. It is easy to grow in moist, rich (but not heavy) soil, which needs digging well and manuring prior to planting. One plant will usually produce quite enough horseradish for domestic use, and as it is invasive it should be restrained in some secluded part of your garden. It is very hardy down to at least 10°F (−12°C), US zones 8–10.

Lovage

A handsome robust perennial found throughout Europe, *Levisticum officinale* probably originated from the eastern Mediterranean region. The young shoots are bronze-coloured when they first emerge in early spring and develop into stems up to 7ft (2m) tall, bearing strongly scented, dark green, glossy divided leaves. The small flowers are yellowish green, borne in clusters in summer and are followed by ovoid brown fruits. The plant's overpowering smell of celery was rather unkindly described by Dr Martyn in 1807 as 'strong and peculiarly ungrateful'. It also tastes like celery but with a distinct yeastiness. All parts of the plant can be used for flavouring soups, stews and other meat dishes. Lovage was much used by the Romans in many recipes, and was cultivated in monastic gardens throughout Europe. The ground seed can be added to bread, cakes and pastries, while the roots have a slightly nutty flavour and can be peeled (the skin tastes bitter) and eaten as a vegetable or grated into salads. The stems can be blanched by earthing up, and used in the same

way as celery. The leaf stalks can be used in the same way as angelica. To maintain a good supply of young leaves and stalks cut some stems back down to ground level throughout the season.

PLANTING HELP Lovage can be grown from ripe seed sown outside in the autumn, or dried seed indoors in the spring. Another method of propagation is to divide and replant the fleshy rootstocks in spring. Grow in sun or semi-shade in good, deep, well-drained, moisture-retaining soil, and mulch with manure if you can. Remember that it will make a tall plant, so find a place for it at the back of the border and be prepared to stake it if it is in an exposed position. If left undisturbed in good conditions, it will last for several years. It can also be grown in a large pot, although it will probably need trimming back as it is apt to become rather untidy. It is very hardy, down to at least 10°F (−12°C), US zones 8–10.

Thyme
(*See page 8*)

Lovage

Borage *Borago officinalis*

Borage

Borage

An annual native to S Europe, *Borago officinalis* is naturalized in other regions of Europe and parts of North America. It is a robust plant with round, hollow stems growing up to 2ft (60cm) and is covered with bristly hairs. Borage has large, dark green oval leaves and attractive, star-shaped electric blue flowers from summer through to the first autumn frosts. Although it is an annual, borage self-seeds freely and will often come up year after year in the same part of the garden. The white-flowered form **'Alba'** is seen occasionally and can be used in the same way as the blue form.

The pretty blue flowers are much used in Britain in the summer months to adorn jugs of Pimms. The flowers can also be used to decorate fruit or green salads, or crystallized and used as

cake decorations. Elizabeth David reported that the Italians use it in ravioli, and also fry the leaves in batter and serve as sweet fritters. The young leaves have a light, cucumbery taste which combines well with lemon and sugar to make long summer drinks, or they can be shredded and used in salads or cooked in the same way as spinach. They can also be used in fish and aspic dishes or added to pea and bean soups, and are a useful ingredient of vegetable stocks. The leaves are a good source of potassium and calcium. Both leaves and flowers are best used fresh.

PLANTING HELP   Borage is best grown from seed sown *in situ*, as it has a long taproot and dislikes being disturbed. If you are desperate for an early crop, however, it is possible to start the seed off in plug trays under glass, so that the seedlings can be planted out without disturbing the roots once the danger of frost has passed. Borage does best in well-drained soil, preferably in a sunny part of the garden. It is an untidy, sprawling plant, with a tendency to self-seed, so allow it plenty of room, and be prepared to pull up seedlings. Hardy to 0°F (−18°C), US zones 7–10.

Mallows

Mallow *Malva verticillata* An annual plant native to E Asia that was grown in European vegetable gardens in the past and is still cultivated in China and South Africa. It makes a rosette of long-stemmed leaves before sending up a tall branching flowering stem up to 7ft (2m), which bears small white or lilac flowers. All parts of the plant are edible when young. The leaves can be picked as required and eaten in soups or lightly boiled like spinach. The variety **'Crispa'**, which has pale lilac flowers and leaves with a particularly crinkly edge can be added to salads.

Apicius gives a recipe for a dish of peas and beans in which mallow flowers are included, and there are a number of other Roman recipes in which it is an ingredient. Mallow leaves are the basis of a soup – popular in the Middle East, especially Egypt – called *Melokhia*; Claudia Roden gives a recipe for this in her book. The proper plant for this purpose is *Corchorus olitorius*, which has broad toothed leaves and small yellow flowers. It grows in warm climates, but in cold climates the mallows described here are used as substitutes.

PLANTING HELP Annual Mallows are easy to grow from seed sown in spring *in situ* and thinned to about 8in (20cm) apart. They do well in good, well-drained soil in full sun. Mallows are hardy down to 10°F (−12°C), US zones 8–10.

Marsh Mallow *Althaea officinalis* A tough perennial found in damp grassy places, especially near the sea in Europe and northern Asia. The thick roots are full of mucilage and is used to make the sweets of the same name. These were particularly popular in Asia Minor in Roman times. In France the young shoots and tender leaves are also eaten raw in salad.

Marsh Mallow *Althaea officinalis* at Wisley

Borago officinalis 'Alba'

Malva verticillata 'Crispa'

Landcress *Barbarea species*

Wild landcress run to seed

Landcress

American Cress, Belle Isle Cress, Yellow Rocket, Winter Cress *Barbarea species* A low-growing biennial herb, of which there are several different but very similar species native to Europe, and naturalized in North America. They make plants up to about 2½ft (75cm) tall with rosettes of glossy, dark green divided leaves and bright yellow flowers (similar in appearance to mustard) in spring. The young leaves have a hot, peppery taste similar to that of watercress and are particularly useful as they can be harvested throughout the winter when other green herbs are scarce. Protection with cloches during cold weather, while not necessary for the maintenance of the plant, will prevent the leaves from becoming tough. They are useful for pepping up salads and sandwiches and can also be used as a garnish for soups. When the weather becomes warmer, the plant tends to run to seed very quickly, and once that has happened the leaves become too hot and bitter to use.

Landcress has long been grown as a herb and salad plant. Its use declined in England during the 18th century, but it remained popular in America, and has now made a comeback in Britain.

PLANTING HELP   Landcress does best in a good moisture-retaining soil in sun or semi-shade; it should not be allowed to dry out. Although strictly speaking a biennial, it is usually grown as an annual. Seed should be sown at a depth of about ⅓in (1cm) *in situ* in spring, or in summer for overwintering. Germination can be slow in dry weather, but can be helped by frequent watering. Landcress is extremely hardy once established, down to 10°F (−12°C), US zones 8–10, and can usually be relied on to produce leaves throughout the winter.

Rocket

Both types of rocket described here are best grown from seed sown *in situ* in good moist soil in open ground in spring (once all danger of frost has passed), or in mild areas, in autumn for overwintering. Wild rocket will

Salad Rocket

tolerate drier conditions than Salad Rocket and is also hardier. The first leaves are ready to harvest after about 6 weeks and must be picked frequently to ensure a good supply. It is possible to cut the plants right down to the ground several times during the season, as they will shoot up again if the soil is moist enough. Try to avoid a situation in full sun or the plants will dry out and flower too soon. Once this happens the quality of the leaves starts to deteriorate and their flavour becomes unpleasantly strong.

Salad Rocket, **Roquette** or **Arugula** *Eruca vesicaria* subsp. *sativa*   A rather tender annual herb whose exact origins are unclear, although it is native to the Mediterranean region and widely naturalized throughout N Europe. It is known to have been cultivated by the Romans and has a long history of culinary use in S Europe; it has recently become very popular in Britain and North America. The young leaves are widely used as an ingredient of salads, their peppery flavour adding piquancy.

PLANTING HELP   The plants grow quickly, with long thin stems up to about 2ft (60cm) tall, bearing deeply lobed leaves in the wild seed variety and unlobed or only occasionally lobed leaves in the cultivated type, with white, cream or yellowish flowers with reddish purple veins, which are also edible and can be added as a garnish to salads. As with landcress, the plants will quickly run to seed in hot weather, rendering the leaves inedible, although the advantage is that you can save seed for sowing yourself. Hardy to 0°F (−18°C), US zones 7–10.

Wild or **Perennial Wall Rocket**
Diplotaxis tenuifolia
This is a hardy perennial herb native to southern and central Europe, and found growing wild (possibly escaped from gardens) on old walls and waste ground in Britain. It has a long taproot, and produces long branching stems that grow to about 2½ft (75cm) tall, bearing bright yellow, sweetly honey-scented flowers during summer and autumn. The leaves are larger than those of Salad Rocket, but are not good to eat once the plant has flowered as they have a very bitter aftertaste. Hardy to 10°F (−12°C), US zones 8–10.

Wild Rocket

Wild Rocket *Diplotaxis tenuifolia*

Houttuynia cordata 'Chameleon'

Houttuynia cordata

Houttuynia

An evergreen perennial herb, *Houttuynia cordata* is found in damp woodland in most of temperate E Asia. It grows up to about 20in (50cm) tall, making clumps of dark green, heart-shaped leaves and sending out spreading stems; the attractive white 'flowers' (they are really bracts) are followed by a fruit capsule containing numerous small seeds. Three forms are grown in gardens in Europe for their ornamental attributes: the form illustrated here; one with double flowers; and

'**Chameleon**' or '**Variegata**', which has green, red and white variegated leaves. Houttuynia is very popular in China and Japan, where the young leaves and shoots are picked in early spring and eaten either raw in salads or cooked as a vegetable in the same way as spinach. It makes an attractive and unusual addition to the herb garden.

PLANTING HELP Houttuynia can be grown from seed or propagated by division in the spring. It likes very damp conditions, so needs a moist soil in sun or partial shade. It will grow in very shallow water, so can be planted on the margins of a pool or pond. It is inclined to be invasive, but is less so in drier soils. Hardy down to 10°F (−12°C), US zones 8–10 or possibly lower.

Sorrel

There are about 200 species of sorrels and docks, and although many are edible the two species mentioned here are the most frequently grown for culinary purposes. Sorrel has long been used in French cooking, where it is traditionally served with shad, and a good sorrel sauce makes a delicious accompaniment to many other fish and egg dishes. For an easy recipe see *French Provincial Cooking* by Elizabeth David. Deborah Madison gives a delicious recipe for Sorrel-Onion Tart in *The Greens Cookbook*. It is particularly good in soups and salads, and is also a good source of Vitamin C and iron. Sorrel is rarely grown commercially, so make room for a few plants in your herb garden if you can.

Wild Sorrel

Warning: Avoid cooking sorrel in an aluminium pan as the leaves will taste metallic; use stainless steel or enamelled cast iron. People who suffer from arthritis, gout or kidney stones should not eat sorrel to excess, because of its high oxalic acid content.

PLANTING HELP Sorrel is easy to grow. It does best in moist, cool conditions and good, rich (but not chalky) garden soil, while French Sorrel is more drought-tolerant and will thrive in well-drained soil in warmer conditions. Being perennial, it throws up its leaves from the base of the plant each spring and, if regularly picked, will

Garden Sorrel *Rumex acetosa*

provide you with fresh young leaves throughout the year until it is finally cut back by frost.

Sorrel can be divided and replanted in autumn, but is usually grown from seed, sown *in situ* in spring. It should be replaced every few years as it tends to become woody. The leaves can be harvested about eight weeks after sowing. It is very hardy and seldom needs any protection as it dies right down in winter; the protection of a cloche or glass frame will enable you to prolong the harvesting season.

Common or **Garden Sorrel** *Rumex acetosa*
A perennial herb native to hay fields and grassy places throughout Britain and N Europe, which grows up to about 2ft (60cm) tall. The small flowers are green turning to red, and should be removed to prolong the production of young leaves. The leaves, which have arrow-shaped lobes, have an acid flavour and can be braised or puréed and used as a vegetable (similar to spinach) in soups or can be shredded raw and added to salads. Hardy to 10°F (−12°C), US zones 8–10.

French or **Buckler-leaved Sorrel** *Rumex scutatus* A perennial from Europe, Turkey and N Iran, where it grows in rocky places. It spreads by underground shoots, seldom growing to more than 18in (45cm) tall, although it is about 2ft (60cm) wide. The flowers are small and green, turning reddish brown later and are best removed

French Sorrel *Rumex scutatus*

to prolong the production of young leaves. The leaves are shield-shaped (*scuta* means 'shield') and rather smaller and more succulent than those of Garden Sorrel, although they can be used in the same way. The taste is slightly different being more lemony and less acidic. It is particularly popular in France, where it is used as the main ingredient for a soup, also in omelettes and as a sauce for fish and egg dishes. Hardy to 10°F (−12°C), US zones 8–10.

Crisped-leaf
Parsley

Parsley

One of the most popular and well-known
of all herbs, parsley is not only delicious
but is also a good source of vitamins,
especially vitamin C. It is not known as a wild
plant, although it is thought to be native to
S Europe but it has escaped from gardens in many
places so is often found growing wild. It was
known and used as a herb by the Greeks, and
Theophrastus, writing in about 320 BC, mentioned
two varieties. It was cultivated from then onwards
and may have been brought to Britain by the
Romans. It was widely grown in Britain by the
mid-14th century and by 1656 Tradescant was able
to list seven varieties of parsley growing in his
garden at Lambeth, London.

There are three forms of parsley used in the
kitchen today: Crisped-leaf Parsley, Flat-leaved
Parsley and Hamburg Parsley. All three are
biennials, easily grown in good soil and very hardy.
Parsley leaves have a pleasant taste, look attractive
as a garnish and are used in salads, stuffings and
sauces throughout much of the world. On several
occasions, when travelling in central Asia, we have
been given huge platefuls of green salads, with
Flat-leaved Parsley as the main constituent.

PLANTING HELP   New varieties of parsley
appear all the time and many seed catalogues
contain a bewildering variety to choose from. In
our experience most are perfectly satisfactory, the
main difference between them being the ease
(or otherwise) of germination and the degree of
hardiness. Certain types, for instance 'Moss
Curled' will die down for only a few weeks in a
mild winter before shooting forth again in the
spring. Parsley can be dried, but not very
satisfactorily; freezing is a better method of
preserving its flavour and colour.

Parsley is not difficult to grow, but the seeds are
often slow to germinate (sometimes taking up to
six weeks). To overcome this problem, soak the
seeds in warm water overnight before sowing and
make sure that you use only fresh seed, as it does
not keep well. Sow once the soil has really warmed
up *in situ* in good, moisture-retaining soil, and
water well if the weather is dry until the young
plants have appeared. Thin the seedlings to about
6in (15cm) apart. In very dry weather you will
need to continue watering throughout the summer
to prevent premature seeding and you should also
cut off any stems that start to shoot up to flower in
the first year. The important thing to remember is
that although parsley is a biennial, it needs to be
treated as an annual to ensure a good continuity of
fresh young leaves in the garden. By sowing seed
every year, you should have plants to give you a
good crop of leaves in the current year and
through to the following spring, before running to
seed in the second summer, by which time the
second batch of plants should be in full
production. For a supply of fresh parsley leaves in
winter, either cover the plants with cloches or sow
seed straight into pots (parsley does not transplant
well) in the summer and grow them on ready to
use in the winter.

Naturalized parsley at St Michael's Mount

Flat-leaved and 'Moss Curled' Parsley

PARSLEY

Crisped-leaf Parsley *Petroselinum crispum* used as an edging plant

Crisped-leaf Parsley *Petroselinum crispum*
This type of parsley is the most commonly grown and used in Britain, where it is well adapted to the climate. It probably originates from SE Europe or W Asia, but has escaped from gardens and is naturalized throughout nearly all temperate regions, where it is found growing in rocky waste places and on walls, often near the sea. It can grow to about 2ft (60cm) tall, but is often shorter, and makes a stout plant with a strong taproot and bright green leaves. In summer it bears heads of tiny yellowish flowers.

Crisped-leaf Parsley is used in stuffing for poultry, in dumplings, to make sauces to accompany fish or broad beans and boiled gammon and is also sprinkled on salads. It can also be used as a flavouring for cream cheese, omelettes, rice dishes and so on. Indeed, the possibilities are endless and as a result is one of the herbs that is essential for any garden or patio.
Hardy to 0°F (−18°C), US zones 7–10

'Envy'

The following are some of the varieties of Crisped-leaf Parsley that we have grown ourselves but there are many other varieties available.

'Envy' A variety with dark green leaves, this has proved very hardy in our garden, producing leaves throughout most of the winter.

'Green Velvet' Very similar to 'Moss Curled'.

'Moss Curled' One of the best and most reliable varieties of Crisp-leaved Parsley, this is good for overwintering.

'Green Velvet'

PARSLEY & HAMBURG PARSLEY

Flat-leaved Parsley *Petroselinum crispum* var. *neapolitanum*

Flat-leaved Parsley

Flat-leaved, Italian
or **Plain-leaved**
Parsley *Petroselinum crispum*
var. *neapolitanum*   Also known as
Sheep's or Common Parsley, this
variety is popular in Asia, France, and SE
Europe. The Turks are especially fond of it
and use it to flavour tomato salads; they also
consider it an aphrodisiac. It has a stronger flavour
than the curled varieties and is much used in
Italian cooking, particularly for stuffing
aubergines and courgettes. It is hardier than the
Crisped-leaf types, down to 0°F (−18°C), US
zones 7–10.
Warning: Beware of eating wild parsley found in
roadside ditches or damp woods because it is
likely to be the very poisonous Hemlock Water
Dropwort (*Oenanthe crocata*), which looks similar
and can only be differentiated by its smell of
angelica; if in doubt, do **not** eat it.

Hamburg Parsley
Petroselinum crispum 'Tuberosum'

Parcel

Hamburg Parsley

Although an old variety, popular in E Europe, Hamburg Parsley *Petroselinum crispum* 'Tuberosum' seems not to have been grown in Britain until 1727, when Philip Miller of the Chelsea Physic Garden brought seeds back from Holland. It has leaves similar to Flat-leaved Parsley, but the root is swollen and rather similar in appearance to a parsnip, and can be cooked and eaten as a vegetable. The sweet nutty flavour is delicious. To prepare the roots for cooking, scrub off any earth and either use them whole or cut them into pieces and place in water acidulated with lemon juice (or a drop of vinegar). They can then be roasted and served with meat or turned into chips or fritters, garnished with their own leaves. They are good in casseroles or soups and are traditionally used as an ingredient of Borsht, a Russian beet soup.

PLANTING HELP   Hamburg Parsley is no more difficult to grow than ordinary parsley, but it should be planted in late spring once the soil has warmed up, in deep, stone-free, well-cultivated soil to enable the roots to develop sufficiently for eating. As with other root vegetables, slugs are frequently a problem and if given the chance will attack the roots, so be on the lookout for them, and, if necessary, put out a 'slug-pub' (a jar with dregs of beer) near the plants. Hamburg Parsley is hardier than the Moss-curled varieties, and can be useful in winter when you may find a few small leaves poking out of the ground in even the coldest weather. Hardy to 0°F (−18°C), US zones 7–10.

Parcel

This is a new variety of celery, marketed by the seed firm Thompson and Morgan as Parcel (Zwolse Krul). It looks like a parsley but tastes like celery, with the younger, lighter green leaves being the best, as the older ones sometimes become rather bitter and slightly tough. We have grown it for a year now and found it very useful; it seems very tolerant, having withstood a dry summer and cold frosty spells in the winter. It has produced leaves constantly throughout this time without dying down at all, finally flowering in the second summer. It is good in salads and as a replacement for ordinary parsley in sauces and soups.

PLANTING HELP   Sow the seeds in early to mid-spring in good seed compost, keeping at 70°F (21°C) until germination, which takes 2–3 weeks. Transplant the seedlings into small pots and start to acclimatize them to cooler conditions, and plant outside once all risk of frost has passed. It will tolerate sun or light shade. To grow Parcel as a pot plant, simply pot on into bigger pots and grow in a light but cool, airy place. Hardy to 0°F (−18°C), US zones 7–10.

Chervil

An annual herb native to S Europe and W Asia, *Anthriscus cerefolium* is now found naturalized in many areas growing in hedgerows and grassy places. It grows to about 2ft (60cm) tall, and has bright green, feathery leaves (similar to Cow Parsley, to which it is related) and clusters of small white flowers. It has a long history of cultivation, and Gerard in his *Herball* of 1636 described the leaves as 'exceeding good, wholesome and pleasant', and the roots 'likewise most excellent in a sallad, if they be boiled and afterwards dressed'.

Chervil

The sweetly aromatic leaves, which are best picked when young, are used chopped and sprinkled onto salad and vegetable dishes, as well as in soups, sauces, poultry, egg and fish dishes. Its delicate flavour is akin to parsley with overtones of aniseed. Nika Hazelton, in *Danish Cooking*, gives a delicious recipe for chervil soup, which is served with poached eggs; she warns against boiling the soup once the chervil has been added, as the delicate taste and colour of the herb will be lost. For both coriander and chervil you must use freshly picked leaves if possible as they wilt quickly, and if adding to cooked food leave until the last minute as the flavour disappears rapidly. The leaves should not be dried but can be frozen satisfactorily. The roots can be cooked and served hot or cold, as a vegetable, but of course this necessitates the lifting of the whole plant in the summer, thus robbing you of the leaves.

PLANTING HELP   Sow seed *in situ* (chervil dislikes being transplanted) in moisture-retaining but not waterlogged soil, in succession, from spring through summer to provide a continuous supply of fresh young leaves. Chervil prefers cooler climates and should not be allowed to dry out, as the plants will 'bolt' into seed very quickly. It can be grown in pots either indoors or out, and can therefore be brought indoors for the winter, although it is hardy down to about 10°F (−12°C), US zones 8–10.

Chervil *Anthriscus cerefolium* in an old pot with mint behind

Coriander *Coriandrum sativum* in flower

Coriander *Coriandrum sativum*

Coriander seeds

Coriander

Chinese Parsley, **Cilantro** *Coriandrum sativum*
A very aromatic annual herb native to the
Mediterranean region. It grows up to about 20in
(50cm) tall and produces two kinds of leaves, the
lower ones being quite broad with serrated edges,
while the upper ones are feathery and have a
stronger scent. Small white, pale pink or lilac
flowers are produced in clusters during the
summer. Both the seeds and the leaves have a very
distinctive taste, and are frequently used in
Oriental, Caribbean, and South American
cooking. It is very popular in India where the
leaves are used as a garnish and the ground seeds
are used to flavour curries. Madhur Jaffrey, in her
book *Indian Cookery*, suggests serving fresh
coriander leaves with mackerel and ground
coriander seeds with turnips.

The plant has a long culinary history in Europe
and was brought to Britain by the Romans. It has
become deservedly popular again with the fresh
leaves and young plants freely available in
greengrocers and supermarkets. Pick the young
leaves when they are required and add them raw
to salads, sauces and egg dishes. Coriander leaves
also impart a delicious flavour to certain kinds of
meat, especially lamb, although it is usually best to
add them just before serving, rather than to cook
them. If you want to harvest the seeds, pull up the
whole plant when the fruits begin to turn grey
brown and treat as for caraway (*see page 68*).

PLANTING HELP Grow from
seed sown *in situ* during spring and
summer in light, finely raked, well-
drained soil and, for best results,
give it a warm sunny spot. Thin
the seedlings to about 4in
(10cm) apart or less if only the
leaves are wanted. If keeping
the plants for seed support
them with canes or pea
sticks to prevent the plants from
collapsing. Coriander is not
particularly hardy, and you are unlikely
to be able to overwinter it unless you live
in a very mild climate, so it is best simply
to treat it as an annual. Hardy down to
about 20°F (–6°C), US zones 9–10.

Coriander

Caraway

A hardy biennial herb native to
S Europe, NW Africa and
parts of Asia, as far north as
the Himalayas, *Carum carvi*
is also occasionally found
naturalized in Britain. It
makes a small plant in the
first year, but if kept for a
second season will eventually
grow up to 2ft (60cm) tall. It has
light green, feathery foliage and
little clusters of pinky white flowers
in early summer. Now grown commercially in
many parts of the world, it has long been used for
culinary and medicinal use. In Victorian England
it became particularly associated with 'seed cake'
and was also used to make sweet toppings for Bath
buns, although the English taste for caraway seems
to have faded away by the beginning of this
century. This is a pity, as the seeds have a
distinctive flavour and seed cake itself is worth a
try. Jane Grigson gives an easy and delicious recipe
in her excellent book *British Cookery* and the
resulting light, moist cake is a treat, especially if
taken with a glass of Madeira.

The seeds can also be used in savory dishes: to
flavour cabbage, either in sauerkraut or when stir-
fried; or in rich meat casseroles. The young leaves
can also be chopped and used in salads and the
thick roots of two-year-old plants can be cooked
and eaten as a vegetable.

To harvest the seeds, wait until the tips of the
fruits turn almost grey, then cut off the stems, tie
them in bundles, place a brown paper bag over the
seed heads and turn upside down. Leave them in a
dry place indoors for a few days before shaking the
whole bunch vigorously. The seeds can then be
stored in a screw-top glass jar in a dry dark place,
however, the flavour will fade with time.

Caraway seed

PLANTING HELP   Plant seed in spring or
even better in autumn when the seed is fresh, in a
sunny place, in ordinary well-drained soil which
you have raked to a fine tilth. Sow in the sunniest
place you can find and thin the plants out to about
6in (15cm) apart. Caraway is very hardy, down to
−40°F (−40°C), US zones 3–8; you can also treat it
as an annual and sow seed every year.

Cumin *Cuminum cyminum* in flower

Caraway *Carum carvi*

Cumin

An annual from the
Mediterranean region
east to C Asia and south to
the Sudan, *Cuminum
cyminum* is often referred to
as a spice rather than a herb. It is the aromatic
seeds of this plant which are used for cooking.
Cumin is a small slender plant up to 6in (15cm)
tall with very narrow, thread-like green leaves and
heads of small white or pink flowers. Cumin is
rather underrated in W Europe, but it was
commonly used in Britain until the 17th century,

Cumin seed

CUMIN

Cumin growing with an *Agastache*

when it appears to have been replaced in popularity by caraway seed, but thanks to increased interest in international cuisine the seeds are now freely available to the gardener.

Cumin seeds are best used when slightly roasted to impart a warm and pungent flavour to curries, pickles and stuffings. They are much used in Indian and North African cooking, and are an essential ingredient of many curry and chili powders including *Garam Marsala*. Madhur Jaffrey uses cumin in some of the recipes in her book *Indian Cookery*, and explains how to roast the seeds. Cumin is very good when used in a marinade with red wine and orange juice to flavour lamb. Deborah Madison in *The Greens Cookbook*, suggests using cumin and mint to make a vinaigrette dressing; the seeds need to be pounded in a mortar. They are also good with stir-fried cabbage, and can be ground and added to

egg dishes; they are used commercially to flavour cheeses and pickles.

PLANTING HELP Sow seeds under glass in spring, planting the seedlings out in good, well-drained soil when all danger of frost has passed and the soil has warmed up. You will only get good ripe seed after a long warm summer, and the weather conditions in N Europe are rarely suitable; placing the plants in a sunny, not baking hot, sheltered spot will help, as will the protection of the young plants with a cloche to begin with. Harvest the whole plant once the seed pods have ripened. Tie the stems in loose bunches, cover the heads with a brown paper bag and hang up to dry in a cool, dry, airy place for a few days. Discard the stems and you should be left with a bag of dry ripe seeds which you can store in an airtight jar. Hardy to about 32°F (−0°C), US zone 10.

Dill *Anethum graveolens*

Dill in the herb garden at Gravetye Manor

Dill

Dillweed *Anethum graveolens* A hardy annual herb which originates from S Europe and parts of W Asia. In favourable conditions it will make a striking bush to about 2½ft (75cm) tall with feathery, bluish green leaves and clusters of tiny yellow flowers in summer. The seeds are dark brown and highly aromatic, and are used commercially in making gripe water for babies. You can use them whole or ground up as an addition to fish dishes; they are particularly good with salmon. The leaves have a milder flavour and a particular affinity with fish, and are used to make Gravad Lax and other Scandinavian pickled fish dishes. They are also delicious with cucumber (Nika Hazelton gives a very good recipe for pickled cucumber in her book of *Danish Cooking*) and gherkins, or dill pickles.

The leaves can be dried and are a useful addition to the store cupboard. They can be used to make dill bread for which there is an excellent recipe in *The Greens Cookbook*.

To harvest the seeds, either pull up the entire plant or cut it off at ground level as soon as the flower heads turn brown, otherwise you will lose the seed. Tie the stems in loose bunches, cover the heads with a brown paper bag and hang up to dry in a cool (but not damp), airy place for a few days. Discard the stems and you should be left with a bag of dry ripe seeds which you can store in an airtight jar.

PLANTING HELP Sow seed in spring *in situ* in ground that has been thoroughly cleared of weeds; the tiny seedlings, which should be thinned to about 1ft (30cm) apart, will not survive if there is competition. Try and provide a sunny, well-drained site with shelter from the wind, but do not allow to dry out in hot weather or the plant will run to seed very quickly. Hardy down to about 32°F (0°C), US zone 10.

Fennel

A hardy perennial originating from Europe and the Mediterranean region, *Foeniculum vulgare* is naturalized in parts of Britain, usually by the sea. It makes a graceful plant up to about 5ft (1.5m) tall and has greyish green branched, hollow stems and fine, soft green leaves. The tiny yellow flowers (which are very similar to those of dill) are borne in clusters and are followed by seeds, which, when dried, can be used for flavouring bread, cakes and biscuits; in Italy they are added to sausages and stuffings. Both the leaves and the stems (which are best peeled), have an aniseed flavour and can be harvested throughout the summer and added to

FENNEL

Fennel at Joy Larkcom's potager in Suffolk

Florence Fennel

fish and poultry dishes, vegetables and salads. It takes pride of place in the Provençal dish known as *Grillade au Fenouil*, in which seabass or red mullet is grilled (and finally, and dramatically, flambéed) over a bed of dried fennel stalks (Elizabeth David has a recipe for this). Keep cutting back some stems to provide a supply of leaves. The leaves can be satisfactorily frozen. Hardy to 10°F (−12°C), US zones 8–10.

Bronze Fennel *Foeniculum vulgare* 'Purpurascens' A decorative form with purplish-bronze foliage which can be used to add colour and flavour to salads and fish dishes.

Florence Fennel or **Finocchio** *Foeniculum vulgare* var. *azoricum* A lower-growing form of fennel that has swollen white leaf bases which form what we call the bulb. It is grown as an annual or biennial, and is the fennel much used in Italy and elsewhere for cooking as a vegetable (it is particularly delicious when roasted) or for use shredded raw in salads. There are several named cultivars of Florence Fennel and there is also another form, *F. vulgare* var. *dulce*, with smaller, thinner bulbs. The feathery leaves can be used in the same way as Common Fennel.

PLANTING HELP Fennel can be sown from seed or propagated by division in the spring, while Florence Fennel is grown each year from seed sown *in situ* in late spring, once all danger of frost has passed. A warm sunny position in deep, well-drained soil will give the best results, and should

Bronze Fennel at Eden Croft Herb Garden, Kent

be given plenty of water during hot weather in order to plump up the bulb. It is not always easy to grow Florence Fennel in Britain and N Europe, because it requires a long, warm summer to mature, but we have found that even small bulbs have a good flavour, so it is worth a try. Once the root base of Florence Fennel starts to swell it should be earthed up to blanch it. Fennel dies down in the winter and will normally withstand temperatures at least as low as 10°F (−12°C), US zones 8–10.

Clipped bay *Laurus nobilis* at Portmeirion, North Wales

Bay

Bay Laurel *Laurus nobilis*   This noble evergreen tree or shrub deserves a place in every garden, and not only for its culinary usefulness, but also because of its attractive habit of growth. Being a tree or large bush, it lends height and structure to a herb garden, which might otherwise be very much all on one plane. Although one plant will provide ample leaves for domestic use, it is tempting to include more if you have sufficient space. It has glossy dark green leaves and small greenish yellow flowers that appear during late summer or autumn, and are followed (in mild areas only) by shiny black round berries. Bay leaves are an essential part of *bouquet garni* which is used in many recipes and they add a distinctive taste

Bay leaves

to casseroles. Bay imparts a wonderful flavour to herb marinades for fish and chicken dishes, and I always add a leaf when boiling bacon or gammon or poaching salmon. Infuse a leaf in the milk or stock used in roux-based sauces for added flavour.

It is native to the Mediterranean region, but has long been cultivated elsewhere (it had been introduced to Britain by the 16th century). The Romans enjoyed the distinctive flavour and Apicius suggested that sausages should be wrapped in bay leaves before being hung up to smoke. The leaves can be used fresh throughout the year, but have a more pronounced flavour when dried.

It is really worth investing in a small specimen, which should live for many years. Bay is easy to grow, preferring a well-drained but moisture-retentive soil and a sunny position, but make sure there is room for growth, as it can eventually make a very large plant. It does well in containers and in formal gardens is often clipped into very attractive ornamental shapes. Plants in pots are more susceptible to cold damage, so be ready to bring the plant under cover during very cold weather.

PLANTING HELP   Bay is not easy to propagate, which is a good reason for leaving it to

Lemon Verbena *Aloysia triphylla* flowering outdoors at Ventnor Botanic Garden, Isle of Wight

the professionals. However, if you are determined to do it yourself, it is possible to grow plants from cuttings taken in late summer. Bay may grow up to 45ft (20m) tall, but is normally grown as a bush of about 7–10ft (2–3m). In very cold weather it may be cut back by frost, but will often sprout up again the following spring. Bay is hardy down to 10°F (−12°C), US zones 8–10 in a protected site.

Lemon Verbena

A slightly tender deciduous shrub, growing up to about 16ft (5m) tall, *Aloysia triphylla* (syn. *Lippia citriodora*) originates from Chile. It was introduced into Britain at the end of the 18th century and has long been grown in conservatories or cool greenhouses. The plants can live a long time; we know of one specimen which has been growing happily on a wall in a cool greenhouse for over 40 years. The long, fairly narrow, powerfully scented leaves are pale green and slightly sticky, and the clusters of tiny lilac-coloured flowers appear in late summer. Lemon Verbena leaves are best used fresh and can be added to summer drinks, fruit dishes, puddings – almost anything that would benefit from lemon flavour. They can also be dried and used for culinary purposes or added to pot pourris.

PLANTING HELP   In mild coastal areas Lemon Verbena can be grown satisfactorily in the open, but in cooler climates the protection of a south-facing wall is necessary. In areas where temperatures regularly fall below freezing it is best

treated as a greenhouse plant. It can be grown outside in a large pot, which can be brought indoors in cold weather. It should be given a warm, sunny position in well-drained soil, and, if outside, should be protected from frost with fleece or a good layer of straw or bracken. Do not panic if the shoots are late in appearing in the spring, they will struggle through eventually and any dead bits can then be trimmed off.

Cuttings can be taken in early summer and rooted indoors (preferably with bottom heat) and the young plants can then be grown on and gradually hardened off for outdoor planting. Pinch out the tops of young plants to encourage branching and cut back wall-trained specimens quite hard in spring. Hardy to 20°F (−6°C), US zones 9–10.

Lemon Verbena

Myrtle *Myrtus communis*

Myrtle

Common Myrtle *Myrtus communis*
This attractive, fragrant evergreen shrub is
probably native to the Mediterranean region,
although it has been cultivated for so long that its
exact origins are obscure. Since Classical times it
has been a symbol of love and a sprig was
traditionally included in a bride's bouquet. The
berries were used as a spice by the Greeks and
Romans – Apicius included them in recipes for
preserving turnips, sausages, a dressing to
accompany boiled partridge and a sauce for boar.
They can be used as a substitute for juniper
berries to decorate pâtés and pies or, when ground
and deseeded, to flavour venison and many other
meat dishes.

Myrtle can grow up to about 13ft (4m) or more,
and, like bay, is an attractive addition to the
garden, bringing height and, if clipped, an element
of formality. It has reddish bark that becomes grey
and cracked with age and small dark green, glossy
leaves which are aromatic when crushed. The
attractive white scented flowers appear in summer
and are followed by deep blackish purple berries.
It is very tolerant of clipping and can be trimmed
into formal shapes if required; in any case it

benefits from trimming back in spring once the
danger of frost is past. Myrtle can be propagated
by cuttings taken in spring and summer and
placed in compost under glass. It can also be
propagated by layering, but as you will probably
only need one plant it is better just to buy one
from your local nursery.

Myrtus communis
ssp. *tarentina*

Common Juniper *Juniperus communis*

PLANTING HELP Myrtle is best given the protection of a south-facing wall in Britain and N Europe. It does best in a good well-drained soil, with the addition of well-rotted leaf mould or household compost. It can be grown in a large pot successfully and if you live in an area subject to frost it would be the best way of growing it as it can then be brought indoors for the winter. In a sheltered place, if protected with fleece, it is hardy down to about 10°F (–12°C), US zones 8–10.

Myrtus communis subsp. *tarentina* A more compact form with smaller leaves growing eventually up to about 5ft (1.5m). It has whitish berries which are seldom produced in Britain and N Europe as the growing season is too short, but successful in warmer climates such as California.

Juniper

Common Juniper *Juniperus communis* This evergreen shrub is native throughout much of the Northern Hemisphere and is widely distributed. Juniper is found in Britain growing on chalk downland and limestone hills. It can grow up to about 10ft (3m) or more, and in sheltered spots will make a tree as high as 40ft (12m), but in exposed positions it can be much lower than this. The small leaves are green, needle-like and very aromatic. The flowers are tiny and insignificant and the fruits are round berries,

Juniper berries

containing two or three seeds, which are green, turning black when ripe. In addition to the species described here, there are many named garden varieties, most of which differ little from the original form, and these can be used as substitutes if necessary.

Juniper berries are used to flavour gin and a type of Norwegian beer. Its distinctive taste adds zest to marinades and stuffings and it is useful in venison, game and pork dishes, especially casseroles. It also enhances bean dishes, cabbage, duck and goose. To obtain berries you will need one male and one female plant; the male flowers are small, egg-shaped and catkin-like, while the females are small and berry-like, and turn into the fruits. Pick the berries when they have turned colour towards the end of the summer, spread them out thinly on a tray and dry. **NB**: It is unwise for pregnant women or those with kidney disease to eat the berries since they act as a diuretic.

PLANTING HELP The Common Juniper will thrive in well-drained soil and tolerates chalky or limy soils. To keep the plants in shape, trim back gently but do not cut into the old wood. Juniper can be grown in tubs or pots and is tolerant of dry conditions. It can be grown from seed sown in the autumn, but germination can take an exceedingly long time. One way to speed up the process is to plunge the seeds into boiling water for a few seconds prior to sowing; it is easier to propagate from cuttings in the spring or autumn. Juniper is extremely tough and will tolerate temperatures down to 0°F (–18°C), US zones 7–10.

Garlic *Allium sativum* in a Chinese market

Garlic

A bulbous plant, sometimes growing up to 2½ft (75cm) tall, *Allium sativum* has several flat green leaves and a bulb with a white or pale pink paper-like covering, which breaks up into cloves. It is not known as a wild plant, but is probably derived from the wild onion *Allium longicuspis* from central Asia. It is one of the most popular and well-known of all the herbs and spices, having been used since the time of the first Egyptian dynasty 3000 years before Christ and possibly earlier. It is esteemed for its medicinal and culinary properties and all sorts of extravagant claims have been made as to its efficacy in promoting good health. It is much used in Mediterranean and E European cooking and is also an essential ingredient of most Chinese dishes. It is particularly good when added to otherwise rather bland dishes such as chicken and white fish and is also valuable in salad dressings. Both children and adults find garlic bread delicious and easy to make.

The bulbs are usually harvested during late summer when the leaves have died down, but in some countries it is lifted when immature and the leaves and stem as well as the bulb, are used.

Garlic is grown commercially in large quantities in countries such as France, Italy and Spain and also in California. Jane Grigson gives a wonderful description of the garlic and basil fair at Tours in her *Vegetable Book* and she provides a recipe for *Soupe au pistou*, in which garlic plays an important part.

PLANTING HELP   Garlic is normally planted in the spring in climates with a cold winter, or in autumn in Mediterranean regions. Bulbs are broken up into single cloves and set firmly in sandy soil in a warm, sunny place. They should be kept well watered and free of weeds until the tops die back at the end of the summer; some people think that the leaves should be tied up (as with onions) to improve the size of the cloves. Garlic often makes single solid bulbs during the first year, but if kept over winter and planted out the next spring they will form large, multi-cloved bulbs which can then be harvested in late summer and dried in the sun. Store in a cool, dry, airy place to stop the bulbs drying out, a kitchen is usually too hot. Garlic is hardy down to about 10°F (−12°C), US zones 8–10, but needs protection at lower temperatures.

Shallots

Shallots are really small onions and are a subgroup of *Allium cepa* which is the botanical name for onions. They are frequently called for in recipes when an onion flavour is required, particularly in France. We have not included the many varieties of large onion in this book, as we count them as vegetables. Shallots grow as a bunch of bulbs and many of them are old varieties, possibly originating from Ascalon in Palestine, hence the name 'scallion', which is used both for shallots and Welsh Onions. There are many different coloured forms and sizes of shallots, but the grey shallot is particularly highly regarded in France.

Elizabeth David describes shallots as 'one of the most frequently used aromatic vegetables of the French kitchen' and notes that it also 'emulsifies to a greater extent than the onion, which no doubt accounts for its presence as the base of a number of sauces such as *bercy* and *beurre blanc*.' Shallots are also added to casseroles and mixed with chopped mushrooms and onion to form *Duxelles*, which is used as the base for sauces and croquette mixtures.

PLANTING HELP   Be careful to grow members of the onion family on a different site each year so as to prevent the buildup of fungal diseases. Small bulbs (called sets) of shallots are planted in early spring in a sunny, warm place in well-drained, weed-free, sandy soil which should not be manured but can have some bonfire ash dug in to improve the fertility. The bulbs are ready for harvesting in late summer and should be well dried before being stored. They keep better than ordinary onions. Shallots are hardy to 10°F (−12°C), US zones 8–10.

'Hâtive de Niort', a well-known variety of shallot

Babington's Leek

An ancient leek grown by Celtic monks on the western coasts of Europe from the 10th century onwards, *Allium babingtonii* now survives, growing wild on islands and promontories from Ireland to Cornwall. It is derived from the wild leek of southern Europe, *Allium ampeloprasum*, but has, as well as flowers, many small bulbs in the head, which enables it to be propagated after summers too cold and wet for seed ripening.

PLANTING HELP   Its small bulbs enable it to be propagated in wet summers and in colder areas, so it survived far to the north of the range of its parent from the Mediterranean, and is therefore useful in cooler areas. Hardy to about 10°F (−12°C), US zones 8–10.

Babington's Leek on dunes in the Isles of Scilly

Chives

A member of the onion family, *Allium schoenoprasum* is a hardy perennial originating from the mountains of Europe, from Ireland in the west to Siberia, and into Japan in the east. It makes a low clump of narrow, hollow, grass-like leaves, growing up to about 1ft (30cm) tall. The attractive round heads of pale mauve flowers appear during the summer and can be picked and added as a garnish to salads. Cut off the flowers if you wish to use the leaves which are appreciated for their mild onion taste and are added, chopped, to salads of all kinds. They have long been used in such staples as omelettes, baked potatoes, potato salad and egg sandwiches, and are delicious with cream cheese. The leaves can be picked at any time when they are visible, but the plants die down in the winter. The leaves can be dried or frozen, but they are much better when fresh. We have grown chives successfully in pots, but they need quite generous amounts of water and a liquid feed every now and then to keep them going. Refrain from cutting too many leaves at the end of the season, as you will starve the bulbs and they will do badly the following year. There are several varieties in cultivation which differ chiefly in the colour of the flowers and the size of the leaves.

Chinese Chives *Allium tuberosum* in the market in Chengdu

Chives
Allium schoenoprasum

PLANTING HELP
Chives can be grown from seed sown outside once the soil has warmed up, but can also be propagated by dividing clumps of existing plants in spring or autumn, and replanting in a light, rich, moisture-retentive soil. They thrive in cool conditions and are well-suited to the British climate, but even here they require watering in a hot summer. Hardy to −20°F (−29°C), US zones 5–9.

Chinese Chives

Garlic Chives *Allium tuberosum*
This perennial onion has flowering stems up to about 1½ft (45cm) tall and heads of white flowers. It is probably native to China and the eastern Himalayas. It is commonly grown in China for its flat leaves which taste slightly garlicky and are used blanched and eaten as a vegetable; elsewhere the leaves are used green and added to salads in the same way as ordinary chives.

PLANTING HELP   Cultivation is the same as for ordinary chives. Hardy to 0°F (−18°C), US zones 7–10.

Welsh Onion

Japanese Bunching Onion *Allium fistulosum*
A larger, coarser version of chives with hollow evergreen leaves and very little bulb at the base. This perennial plant has been grown in China since prehistoric times, and is widely used in Chinese and Japanese cooking to flavour fried vegetables, but it can also be used raw as a substitiute for chives in the winter. Its association with Wales is a mystery, as it did not reach W Europe until the early 17th century, although some people think it could be derived from the German word *welsche* which means 'foreign'.

Welsh onion *Allium fistulosum*

PLANTING HELP   There are many varieties, some of which are grown as annuals and some as perennials. The perennials can be propagated by taking off the side shoots. They are grown in the same way as Spring Onions and can be blanched by earthing up the soil around the base of the plant. Hardy to 0°F (−18°C), US zones 7–10.

Spring Onion

Scallions, Bunching Onions, Green Onions

Allium cepa   These are simply small specimens of the varieties of common onion, which are used at the stage when they have a long neck and a small bulb. They can be used raw in salads or chopped finely and used in Chinese cooking, particularly in stir-fried dishes, where they are interchangeable with the Welsh onion. In Britain they are frequently encountered as part of a Ploughman's lunch in pubs and are freely available in bunches in shops.

Spring onions in a field trial

PLANTING HELP   Spring onion seed is usually sown during the summer (or autumn in warmer climates) to provide crops for the spring, but it can also be planted during the spring to give a summer harvest. In colder areas the protection of cloches will be needed during the winter. The essence of success is to keep the plants growing as fast as you can, which means watering during dry weather. Hardy to −20°F (−29°C), US zones 5–9.

79

Chop Suey greens *Chrysanthemum coronarium*

but will not tolerate waterlogging. The optimum conditions, however, are light sandy soils and an open sunny situation. If you are making a lawn, you should set the young plants about 6in (15cm) apart and water freely to begin with. Once established it will need very little moisture. If you are using the flowering type, you can sow the seed mixed with silver sand and then treat as above, but the flower heads will need clipping off, otherwise the plants become extremely straggly. We have made a chamomile lawn using 'Treneague' in a London garden which was fairly successful but rather short-lived; planting the dozens of plants required and maintaining them during a hot dry spell was quite an epic feat, so our advice would be not to be too ambitious and start with a seat or path. Chamomile is hardy down to about 10°F (−12°C), US zones 8–10

Chop Suey Greens

Garland Chrysanthemum *Chrysanthemum coronarium*   A native to the Mediterranean region, this annual grows up to about 2½ft (75cm), producing branched stems bearing pale green leaves and, in late summer, yellow daisy-like flowers. Although apparently never used for culinary purposes in S Europe, it is widely cultivated in both China and Japan, where it is used to flavour stir-fried dishes.

Chamomile

Roman Chamomile *Chamaemelum nobile* (syn. *Anthemis nobilis)*   An evergreen perennial growing to about 1ft (30 cm), which originates from W Europe, where it is found growing on grassy heathland. The scent of the feathery aromatic leaves is likened by some to that of apple (literally translated, the name means ground-apple). The attractive yellow-centred white flowers appear in early summer. It is reputed to be a soothing herb and the flowers can be used to make a calming tea, which is conducive to sleep. The Spanish call it *Manzanilla* (little apple) and use it to flavour the eponymous sherry. Because of its reputation as a medicinal herb, it has traditionally been used in the herb garden and often grown as lawns, paths and seats, although for this it is actually best to use the non-flowering form 'Treneague'.

PLANTING HELP   Chamomile can be grown from seed sown under glass in early spring, outside in late spring or propagated by cuttings or division ('Treneague' cannot be grown from seed). It will grow in most reasonable well-drained soils,

PLANTING HELP   Chop Suey greens are easy to grow from seed, which should be sown in spring, and in succession for a good supply of leaves throughout the year. Water in dry weather. Very hardy, down to 0°F (−18° C), US zones 7–10 and continues to grow through the winter.

Chop Suey greens

CHAMOMILE

Chamomile *Chamaemelum nobile*

A chamomile seat made of the non-flowering variety 'Treneague' at Cambridge Botanic Garden

Fenugreek *Trigonella foenum-graecum*

Cardamom

A perennial herbaceous plant originating from India and Sri Lanka, *Elettaria cardamomum* is really thought of as a spice rather than a herb. It is a member of the Ginger family. It makes a plant to 10ft (3m) tall in favourable conditions, with a stout creeping root, narrow leaves and spikes of white flowers striped with pink which are followed by aromatic fruits containing a few small black seeds. It is widely grown in SE Asia, where the fruit capsules are harvested when the plants are about two or three years old. These aromatic seeds, which retain their distinctive flavour better if kept in their capsules and sun-dried, are used for both culinary and medicinal purposes.

Cardamoms are used to flavour curries and other dishes such as stewed fruit (they are particularly delicious with figs), and are used in E Europe to flavour cakes and pastries. Sometimes the whole pod is used and the Turks use it to great effect in flavouring coffee by putting one in the spout of the pot before pouring. In other dishes

Cardamom pods

and spice mixtures the seeds are removed from the pods and finely ground. It is best to store the pods whole in airtight jars, removing the seeds when you require them.

PLANTING HELP This plant cannot be grown outdoors in N Europe, requiring as it does warm conditions; it can be grown in a greenhouse or polytunnel as a curiosity, but unless you are very clever it will not flower and seed here. If you live in a warm climate, such as California, you could try it; it is usually propagated by division, and needs a good, rich soil, and plenty of water and applications of liquid feed while growing, which should be stopped after flowering. It is only hardy to 32°F (0°C), US zone 10.

Fenugreek

A hardy annual, *Trigonella foenum-graecum* is a member of the pea family and is native to the Mediterranean region and naturalized throughout much of S Europe and cultivated in India, Africa and North America, where it grows on hillsides and in dry grassy places. It grows up to 2ft (60cm) and has erect, hollow stems and toothed leaves in groups of three. The scented creamy white flowers appear in summer and are succeeded by long slender pods, containing yellowish brown seeds. The seeds have been used for culinary and medicinal purposes since ancient times and by medieval times it was certainly known in Britain.

Fenugreek is a spicy aromatic plant grown mostly for its seed which is ground up and used to flavour curries, although the fresh green leaves can also be shredded and added to salads; in India they are eaten as a vegetable. The leaves are used to make a tisane and the seeds can be sprouted and have a delicious mild curry flavour and crunchy texture and can be added to salads or served with curries.

To sprout, obtain enough seeds (making sure they are for sprouting and have not been treated with chemicals) to cover the bottom of your container in a shallow layer. Rinse thoroughly, then place in a basin of cold water overnight. Next day, place them in a plastic container and put in a dark, warm place such as an airing cupboard. Rinse every night and morning in clear water to maintain freshness and after four to five days the whole container should be full of crisp, white, sprouted seeds. Once ready, the seeds will not keep for long, but their life can be prolonged for a couple of days by keeping them in the fridge. If you prefer green sprouts, try growing the seeds in the same way as mustard and cress on damp kitchen paper in a shallow dish.

PLANTING HELP   Fenugreek can be sown outside from spring to autumn in good, well-drained but moisture-retaining soil in a sunny place. It will need watering during long dry spells. For a constant supply of young leaves make several successional sowings; the leaves can then be harvested while young and tender. If you are growing this plant for seed, you will need to wait about four months before uprooting and drying it. Fenugreek is easy to grow and is hardy down to about 10°F (−12°C), US zones 8–10.

Turmeric

Another plant which has a pungent flavour and valuable colouring properties, *Curcuma longa* (syn. *Curcuma domestica*) is derived from the root. It is native to India where it is cultivated commercially and for domestic use, as it is in other parts of tropical Asia, and is much used in Indian and Moroccan

cooking. It is similar in appearance to ginger (*see page 86*), the chief difference being that turmeric has broader leaves. It grows up to about 3½ft (1m) and bears greenish pink flowers. The roots (properly called rhizomes) are harvested when the plant is about nine months old and are scalded in hot water to prevent sprouting, peeled and dried ready for use. They are usually used in powdered form, and the bright yellow colour (known as *curcumin*) is used to dye wool, cotton and silk, and to flavour and colour curries. It has been known and valued as a spice and colouring agent for centuries in Britain, Dr Todd Gray recording that the Willoughby family of Leyhill, Devon, included purchases of turmeric in their household accounts in 1650. It can be used as a substitute for saffron, as a colouring and flavouring for rice, chicken and lamb dishes, and in pickles and curry powder. While the colour of turmeric is stable, the flavour soon fades, so only buy small amounts of this spice at a time.

PLANTING HELP   Turmeric is grown from pieces of the root placed in trenches and earthed up with rich soil mixed with manure or compost as the shoots emerge. It requires partial shade and warm, moist but well-drained soil. These conditions are not easy to replicate in N Europe, but it is worth trying in an unheated polytunnel or greenhouse. Plant the rhizomes in the spring once the danger of frost has passed and the soil has warmed up, and keep them watered in hot spells. Dig up the plants in the autumn and wash and dry the rhizomes before storing in a dry place. If you want to keep some plants for the following year, you will need to allow them to be dormant (do not water them) and keep them at a not less than 32°F (0°C), US zone 10.

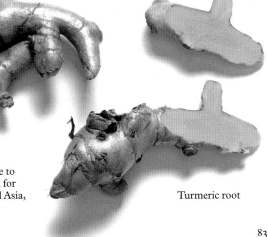

Turmeric root

Wild Saffron *Crocus cartwrightianus*

Saffron

A bulb whose wild origins are unknown, but *Crocus sativus* is thought to be a selection of the wild crocus *Crocus cartwrightianus*, which is native to the Greek islands. It grows up to 8in (20cm) tall and has narrow grass-like green leaves and lilac pink flowers in the early autumn. It is an attractive plant, grown chiefly for its orange red styles, which are used to colour and flavour food. In the past it was widely cultivated throughout Europe; it is clearly depicted on a Minoan vase dating from around 1550 BC and was grown as far north as Saffron Walden in East Anglia in Britain. Today it is grown commercially in the Mediterranean region where the climate ensures reliable flowering.

Saffron is an expensive commodity because at least 100,000 flowers are needed to produce one kilo of dried saffron and the crop cannot be harvested mechanically. Fortunately only small quantities are required for cooking. If you succeed in growing your own supply, you should pick the orange styles as soon as the flowers open and dry them, either in the sun or in a warm place. Once dry, store in airtight containers away from the light to prevent loss of colour.

Elizabeth David recommends that you 'pound up about half a dozen of the little threads, mix them with a couple of tablespoonfuls of the stock of whatever dish the saffron is to flavour, or with water, and leave it to steep until the mixture is an intense bright orange. Then drain this into your rice, soup or whatever it may be and it will dye the whole dish a beautiful pale yellow.'

The pungent spicy taste of saffron is an essential ingredient of bouillabaisse. It is also used in rice dishes, such as *risotto milanese* and *paella*, as well as in breads, cakes and dressings. The American cook Deborah Madison gives an excellent vegetarian recipe for Fettucine and Saffron Butter with Spinach and Roasted Peppers, and another unusual one for Chard and Saffron Tart. Saffron is also used in festive Indian dishes and added to rice dishes such as *Meetha pullao*.

PLANTING HELP   Saffron is fairly easily grown, but is reluctant to flower in N Europe. It does best in a rich, sandy, moisture-retaining but well-drained soil in a warm part of the garden (add some well-rotted farmyard manure before planting if you can). The bulbs (known correctly as corms) should be planted deeply, about 7in (18cm) below the surface and about 6in (15cm) apart in late spring or early summer. The corms will produce smaller corms and, if you manage to keep them that long, will need dividing and replanting about every fourth year. Hardy to −10°F (−23°C,) US zones 6–9.

Safflower

False Saffron, **Kasum** or **Kurdi** *Carthamus tinctorius*   An annual native to W Asia and grown in S Europe, India, China, N Africa and other hot, dry regions of the world. In the past it was exported from N India and Iran to Europe, although some accounts confuse safflower and saffron, making it difficult to trace the plant's history. It has a stiff, stout strong stem that branches near the top and grows up to about 3½ft (1m). The oval green leaves have toothed, spiny edges and the yellow, red or orange flowers bloom from late summer to early autumn. These are followed by small, shiny white fruits.

There are named cultivars available with flowers of varying colours, including white. In some countries, notably India, oil which is low in saturates is obtained from the seed and this is used to make margarines and cooking oils. The plant is also grown for ornamental effect and is used as a dye plant and as a food-colouring agent. Two colours can be obtained from the flowers of this plant, yellow and red; the former is used as a cheaper substitute for saffron (hence the name False Saffron), while the red is used in cosmetics and to dye textiles.

PLANTING HELP   Safflower can be grown from seed under glass in early spring and planted out once all possibility of frost has passed. It needs a light, well-cultivated soil in full sun. Hardy to 20°F (−6°C), US zones 9–10.

Safflower *Carthamus tinctorius*

Lemon Grass

Sayra, **Sereh** *Cymbopogon citratus* A perennial grass which originates from S India and Sri Lanka and is also cultivated in the Seychelles and parts of Africa. It makes a clump of sharply margined, bluish green leaves up to 5ft (1.5m) tall. The leaf bases are whitish green and have a lemony scent and flavour, which is much employed in Chinese cooking and in other parts of Asia as an ingredient of curries and pickles. The stalks can be shredded and used fresh or they can be bought in dried and powdered form. Oil extracted from the leaves is used in perfumery and medicine.

PLANTING HELP Lemon Grass can be grown from seed or by division. It needs a warm, humid atmosphere and should be grown in a good moisture-retentive soil in full sun. It will need the protection of a greenhouse or polytunnel if grown in N Europe, but we have grown it quite satisfactorily inside in a pot under glass. Until recently it was hard to obtain plants in Britain, but with the current interest in Oriental cuisine, this has become easier and a number of specialist herb nuseries now stock it. It needs plenty of water during the growing season and it is best to stand the pot in a saucer of water. It requires a minimum temperature of around 20°F (–6°C), US zones 9–10.

Ginger *Zingiber officinale*

Ginger

Commonly grown throughout the tropics, *Zingiber officinale* is thought to have originated in SE Asia or India, where it has long been cultivated. It is a perennial, growing up to about 5ft (1.5m) tall with pale green leaves and greenish yellow flowers in a cone-like head. The root (rhizome) is used in a number of different ways: fresh (green ginger); dried (root ginger); pickled; or, when immature and preserved in a syrup (stem ginger). It can also be bought in a powdered form. It was valued for its medicinal qualities in the past, but Gerard also noted that it 'is right good with meat in sauces, or otherwise in conditures; for it is of an heating and digesting qualitie'. It has always been an important ingredient of Chinese cooking, particularly in stir-fried dishes (for recipes see the excellent book by Ken Hom). It is also used in curries and to flavour ginger beer, ginger wine, cakes and biscuits, and good quality crystallized stem ginger remains a delicacy.

PLANTING HELP Ginger is grown from pieces of the root placed in trenches and earthed up with rich soil mixed with manure or compost as the shoots emerge. It requires partial shade and warm, moist but well-drained soil, conditions which are not easy to replicate in N Europe. However, it is worth trying in an unheated polytunnel or greenhouse. Plant the rhizomes in the spring once the danger of frost has passed and the soil has warmed up, and keep them watered in hot spells. Dig up the plants in the autumn and wash and dry the rhizomes before storing in a dry place for use. Hardy to 32°F (0°C), US zone 10.

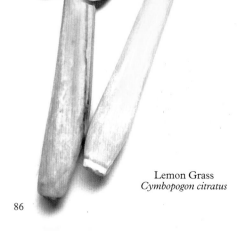

Lemon Grass
Cymbopogon citratus

Liquorice

Like ginger, *Glycyrrhiza glabra* is grown for the flavour of its tuberous root; unlike ginger, it can be successfully grown outdoors in Britain and N Europe. It is a perennial herbaceous plant originating from S Europe and SW Asia, and grows up to about 3ft (90cm) tall with green, almost fern-like leaves and clusters of white or pale blue flowers in late summer, which are followed by small seed pods. The thick, dark reddish brown root, which is yellowish inside, is the part of the plant from which an extract is made and used for culinary purposes. It is dug up about every third autumn, ground into a pulp, boiled in water and evaporated. It is used today in the manufacture of throat pastilles and cough medicine. Tradescant had it in his garden in London in 1656, and it was grown commercially in the liquorice fields of Pontefract in Yorkshire, where it was used to make sweets including Pontefract Cakes, and to flavour beer and stout. Although this industry has now more or less died out in Britain, it is still commercially grown in Russia and some Mediterranean countries.

PLANTING HELP   Liquorice can be propagated by root division, the sections of root being grown at a depth of about 4in (10cm) deep and 2ft (60cm) apart. Once established it will flourish in deep, well-manured and well-drained soil as free from stones as possible (otherwise they interfere with good root growth). When digging up roots for harvesting you can either replant the unwanted roots immediately or store them in a clamp until the following spring. Very hardy to 10°F (−12°C), US zones 8–10 or less.

Liquorice *Glycyrrhiza glabra*

Ginger *Zingiber officinale*

Liquorice *Glycyrrhiza glabra*

Caper *Capparis spinosa* wild near Tarsus, Turkey

Capsicum annuum 'Cayenne'

Caper

A shrubby plant, *Capparis spinosa* is native to the
Mediterranean region where it grows in old walls,
on cliffs and rocky places. It sends out annual
trailing stems with rather thick, greyish-green
leaves, each with a pair of spines at the base. The
attractive large white or pinkish flowers appear in
summer.

Capers have long been grown for their aromatic
buds which are pickled and eaten in sauces such as
Sauce Tartare and Caper Sauce which, in the past
was a popular accompaniment to meat, especially
in Britain. In France, where they are known as
câpres, they are used in Provençal dishes;
according to Elizabeth David the best kind are
distinguished by the wonderful epithet *nonpareilles*
and these come from plants which are grown in
the Var and Bouches-du-Rhône departements of
Provence.

PLANTING HELP   Capers can be grown from
fresh ripe seed or propagated by cuttings, but as
you are unlikely to need more than one bush I
would strongly recommend buying a young plant
which may be difficult in some countries. It
requires a sheltered position in full sun and well-
drained soil as the plant will not tolerate
waterlogging. Capers can be grown outside in the
milder areas of Britain and N Europe, but in
cooler areas will need the protection of a
greenhouse if you wish to obtain any fruit. Hardy
to about 10°F (−12°C), US zones 8–10.

Peppers

Not often included in books on herbs because
peppers *Capsicum annuum* tend to be thought of as
spices, but they are easy and fun to grow, and so
we have decided to include them here. Both the
mild and hot peppers derive from the same species
which is native to Mexico and Central America.
There are two varieties: var. *annuum*, which
includes all the cultivated types; and var.

Banana
Peppers

PEPPERS

Banana Peppers at Villandry, France

minimum, which includes the wild types of pepper that are found growing in the southern United States from Florida to Arizona, and south into South America. The hot varieties, in particular, have been very popular and were dried and powdered and used as a substitute for true pepper, the tropical climber *Piper nigrum*, which was at one time a very expensive commodity from the East Indies.

The hot chilis and other peppers of all types are widely used in Indian, Malaysian and southern Chinese cooking in particular, while the sweet peppers tend to be popular in Mediterranean kitchens. Jane Grigson devoted a section of her excellent *Vegetable Book* to recipes using peppers, both mild and hot, and Elizabeth David also published many recipes in her various books.

PLANTING HELP   Peppers are fast-growing annuals growing best in the hot summers of the tropics. In temperate areas they are best sown under glass in March or early April and when the summer weather comes and all chance of frost has passed they can then be planted out in a hot sunny spot. Hardy to 20°F (–6°C), US zones 9-10. Of the numerous varieties available, we illustrate only a small selection here:

'Cayenne'   A venerable cultivar known since the 16th century and probably earlier, which is nowadays mainly grown in Asia. The long, slender, curved pods are bright red when ripe and are extremely hot. When dried and powdered this and similar cultivars produce the well-known Cayenne pepper, which is used as an ingredient of curry powders and is included in numerous other recipes such as Chicken Gumbo, a recipe from the southern United States.

'Banana Pepper'   One of the types that when dried, is used to make Paprika, an important ingredient of Hungarian Goulash or *Gulyás*. These peppers are generally called **'Sweet Yellow'** or **'Banana'** when they are mild-flavoured, and **'Hungarian Yellow Wax'** when hot. Both types have fruits to about 6in (15cm) long, which are pale yellow when mature, ripening to red in some similar varities.

Paprika

Nasturtium *Tropaeolum majus*

Nasturtium

A popular and vigorous climbing or scrambling annual, *Tropaeolum majus* is native to South America. It has fleshy stems and shield-shaped fleshy green leaves and brightly coloured orange, yellow or red flowers with a spur. Nasturtiums are frequently grown for ornamental purposes (a famous example is Monet's garden at Giverny in France), but they are also useful in summer cooking. The peppery leaves are a good source of vitamin C and iron and can be eaten

Nasturtium

raw in salads, while the flower petals look pretty when scattered over salads. The young buds and green seeds, if pickled in wine vinegar for about a month, can be used as a substitute for capers.

Its smaller relation, *Tropaeolum minus* was brought to Europe from Peru in about 1576 under the name 'Indian Cress' and was given the Latin name *Nasturtium indicum* by John Tradescant in 1656. The name Nasturtium was also applied to watercress, and once you have tasted the peppery leaves and flowers of nasturtium you will see why Tradescant named it thus. The larger-flowered nasturtium *T. majus* was introduced into cultivation in about 1680, and since then the two species have been hybridized. Many named garden varieties, some with variegated leaves, some with different coloured flowers and more compact habit, are now available; all can be used in the same way as the species.

PLANTING HELP Nasturtiums are very easy to grow from seed sown in spring in a warm sunny place in any garden soil, the poorer the better. They are very invasive, scrambling everywhere and seeding themselves with gay abandon, so you will need to think of this when planting. Some kinds have a more pronounced climbing habit than others, and these can be used to great effect against fences and walls, or to cover unsightly

Pot Marigold *Calendula officinalis*

objects during the summer. Save your own seed in the autumn and keep it in envelopes in a dry place for the winter. You will then be able to start a new riot of colour in the spring. Hardy to 32°F (0°C), US zone 10 for short periods.

Pot Marigold

A well-known annual native to C and S Europe and Asia, *Calendula officinalis* is also cultivated in gardens worldwide. It grows to about 18in (45cm) tall with sticky, pale green, oval leaves and attractive bright orange daisy-like flowers throughout summer and until the first frost of autumn. The true Pot Marigold has single flowers but there are varieties with double flowers and numerous named garden varieties. Pot Marigolds are grown for their flowers, which are best used fresh (although they can be dried), and look very attractive when added to salads and fruit salads. They contain *calendulin*, a colouring substance that acts as a substitute for saffron, and as a result marigold is sometimes used to colour rice dishes. The young leaves can be eaten, but I do not advise it as they have a bitter taste.

PLANTING HELP   Marigolds are easily grown from seed sown in spring in any ordinary garden soil, preferably in sun. They germinate quickly and often self-seed. I have seen them covering a large area of a vegetable garden where they were left undisturbed. Marigolds will grow successfully in containers if required, but keep pinching out the tops to stop the plants becoming straggly. Dead-head the flowers to encourage a supply of new blooms. Hardy to −10°F (−23°C), US zones 6-9, for short periods.

Chinese Pepper Tree

Chinese Pepper Tree *Zanthoxylum piperitum*
A shrub or small tree with small, ash-like leaves and greenish flowers followed by small round purplish red fruit. These are commonly used as pepper in China and Japan, and have a strange numbing effect on the mouth if they are chewed. The tree is native to northern China, Japan and Korea, and reaches around 10ft (3m) in cultivation.

PLANTING HELP   Easily grown on the kitchen garden wall or as a small free-standing shrub, hardy to −10°F (−23°C), US zones 6-9.

Chinese Pepper Tree
Zanthoxylum piperitum

Index

INDEX